"A long-overdue resource that is going to be useful for ju.. ...., ... about science."

—**Jonathan Tarbox, PhD, BCBA**, director of the master of science in applied behavior analysis (ABA) program at the University of Southern California, as well as director of research at FirstSteps for Kids

"Amber Valentino has taken the very best of her expertise and experiences and combined it with practical, accessible information to empower ANY post-certification practitioner to conduct applied research. I could almost hear Valentino's voice in my head while I read her book telling me, 'Sarah! You *can* do applied research! Let's go!' I look forward to what will hopefully be an outrageous increase in applied research studies and publications as a result of practitioners using Valentino's book!"

—**Sarah Trautman, MA, BCBA**, cofounder of defy Community, and Amber Valentino's biggest fan

"Research can seem daunting in clinical settings where opportunities and resources may be limited; however, practitioners are in a unique position to conduct socially significant research. Valentino provides practical recommendations, exercises, and examples to help develop research repertoires of practitioners. This book may give you confidence to integrate research into practice—enhancing clinical work, improving outcomes for clients, and pushing the field toward a better understanding of behavior."

—**Jessica Juanico, PhD, BCBA-D**, assistant professor of practice, and assistant director of online programs of applied behavioral science at the University of Kansas

"Valentino makes transparent the spot-on, effective strategies she has used to publish clinical work. I love the conversational style and engaging 'workbook' format of the book, as well as the provided examples. This will be required reading for students in my lab to guide their research projects, because it fills a huge void of behavior analytic texts that support clinicians who want to become a published scientist practitioner."

—**Stephanie M. Peterson, PhD, BCBA-D, LBA**, professor of psychology and associate dean of the college of arts and sciences at Western Michigan University, and editor of *Behavior Analysis in Practice*

"In this book, Valentino presents a straightforward, tried-and-true formula for conducing applied research and closing the research-to-practice gap. It is a must-read for any applied researcher, especially those looking to breakout into the research space."

    —Matthew T. Brodhead, PhD, BCBA-D, associate professor
        at Michigan State University

"As a field, we would greatly benefit from more practicing behavior analysts producing research, but there are very real barriers to doing so. Valentino understands these barriers firsthand, and knows how to overcome them. This handbook is a great how-to guide with activities and worksheets that meet the reader wherever their needs are in starting to produce research. You'll be learning from one of the best with this book!"

    —Daniel Conine, PhD, BCBA-D, assistant professor
        at Georgia State University

"I had the honor to be mentored by Amber Valentino during my postdoctoral fellowship a few years ago. This book is the 'book of wisdom' all postgraduates have been waiting for. Valentino provides a detailed overview of how to design, implement, and publish research with extensive examples that is a breath of fresh air for all practitioners."

    —Angelica A. Aguirre, PhD, BCBA-D, assistant professor
        at Minnesota State University, Mankato

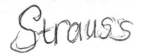

APPLIED BEHAVIOR ANALYSIS

RESEARCH MADE EASY

A Handbook for Practitioners Conducting Research Post-Certification

AMBER L. VALENTINO, PsyD, BCBA-D

02JAN22

CONTEXT PRESS

An Imprint of New Harbinger Publications, Inc.

Distributed in Canada by Raincoast Books

NEW HARBINGER PUBLICATIONS is a registered trademark of
New Harbinger Publications, Inc.

Copyright © 2021 by Amber L. Valentino
          Context Press
          An imprint of New Harbinger Publications, Inc.
          5674 Shattuck Avenue
          Oakland, CA 94609
          www.newharbinger.com

Cover design by Amy Shoup; Acquired by Ryan Buresh;
Edited by Rona Bernstein; Indexed by James Minkin

Library of Congress Cataloging-in-Publication Data

Names: Valentino, Amber, author.
Title: Applied behavior analysis research made easy : a handbook for practitioners conducting research post-certification / by Amber L. Valentino, Psy.D., BCBA-D.
Description: Oakland, CA : New Harbinger Publications, [2021] | Includes bibliographical references and index.
Identifiers: LCCN 2021031169 | ISBN 9781684037827 (trade paperback)
Subjects: LCSH: Psychology, Applied--Research. | Behavior analysts.
Classification: LCC BF636 .V34 2021 | DDC 158.1--dc23
LC record available at https://lccn.loc.gov/2021031169

Printed in the United States of America

23   22   21

10 9 8 7 6 5 4 3 2 1   First Printing

For my husband, Garth, and my son, Porter

Contents

Foreword   vii

Introduction   1

Chapter 1   The Research-to-Practice Gap   9

Chapter 2   Why ABA Practitioners Should Publish   19

Chapter 3   Ethics and Research   44

Chapter 4   Ethical Oversight   55

Chapter 5   Time Management and Staying Productive   74

Chapter 6   Overcoming Obstacles and Barriers   88

Chapter 7   Practical Strategies   102

Chapter 8   Receiving Mentorship   122

Chapter 9   Tips for Writing   133

Chapter 10   A Guide to the Editorial Process   138

Resources   155

Acknowledgments   165

References   167

Index   173

Foreword

The science and practice of behavior analysis is enjoying a heyday, possibly a zeitgeist, or, more modestly, it is coming into its own. For years it was a tiny portion of the vast behavioral and psychological science and practice community. With the rise in the prevalence of autism and the research-verified treatment methods for its symptoms, along with a collection of research-verified treatments for a variety of other mental and behavioral health concerns, its portion of that community has expanded significantly. For a supportive example of what I assert, merely enter "applied behavior analysis" into the search window of the book section of Amazon.com. There are countless books on the science and practice of behavior analysis. However, if one were to search for books explaining how to conduct behavior analytic research and get it published, the search would narrow down to few options. Although these are helpful, they are not as complete nor as uniformly helpful to junior investigators as the book for which this is a foreword.

When I was a graduate student, a dog-eared manual on how to conduct and publish applied behavior analytic research circulated in the department of Human Development and Family Life (HDFL) at the University of Kansas, authored by L. Keith Miller. At that time it was the only book-level resource available that could lead the novice investigator through the publication process. All graduate students in the HDFL department treasured their copy. I certainly treasured mine, although in preparation for writing this foreword, a search of my entire library revealed that my copy has walked off. This is no surprise to me. I have been training behaviorally oriented psychology interns for more than thirty years, and many, probably most, of them have been interested in publishing in behavior analytic journals. Having mastered the process myself, I had no need to consult Keith Miller's guidebook. I suspect one of the former interns borrowed it and now, due to the amnesia that often accompanies borrowed books, they own it (whoever they are). They very likely cherished it and consulted it with vigor as they proceeded with their dissertations or other research projects just as I did back in graduate school. Which brings me to the current offering.

I love this book and wish I would have had it way back in the day, with apologies to Keith Miller. His book was very much a book of its time and indeed was incredibly useful, but the current offering is far more thorough and more directly relevant to the junior investigator. However, I do quibble with the title ever so slightly. I would substitute the word "simple" for "easy" because applied behavior analysis research is not easy. People often mistakenly think simple and easy are synonyms, and they are not. What a heroin addict should do is simple. But it's pretty darn far from easy. What this book has done is simplify the process of doing behavior analytic research and getting it published. It is unlikely to ever be easy—for anyone. Having said that, I assert that simplifying it does indeed make it easier.

And that is a goal that is particularly important for at least three groups of potential consumers: behavior analytic clinicians, behavior analytic students who are in graduate programs that do not supply a complete course on single-subject research design, and non-behavior analytic investigators who would like to conduct single-subject research. This is not to say the book would not be of significant value for seasoned behavior analytic investigators. Having a document that answers virtually every conceivable technical question about publishing applied behavior analytic research at one's fingertips is always a blessing, regardless of one's publishing history. But increasing the publication success of any or all three of these groups serves a larger purpose, specifically the dissemination of the behavior analytic worldview (i.e., the environment is the primary determinant of behavior).

As just one example, behavior analytic clinicians see a broad diversity of clinical conditions and presumably deploy a diversity of interventions to address those problems. At least some of these interventions are very effective, and they include a degree of novelty. Absent an empirically derived published report describing them, knowledge of the interventions is confined to the clinician. But once such a report lands in the pages of a respected peer-reviewed outlet, a portal leading from the clinician to the world at large opens up. Behavior analysts who choose the clinical option for their careers likely bypass many training and educational opportunities whose purpose is to develop research acumen. They presumably seek to expand their clinical acumen instead. Nonetheless, as members of the behavior analytic community they do share the values of that community, a cardinal one of which is appreciation for data-based treatment and decision making. In other words, persuading clinicians to take data on their more interesting cases, especially those that include novel interventions, is not necessarily a tall order. With this book as a resource, they could shape their data-collection methods to match those used by their more research-oriented peers. It is unlikely they would be able to produce extensive lines of systematic investigation, but they could certainly supply well-controlled case studies.

There are vastly more clinicians than researchers in the field of behavior analysis. Thus, the extant body of applied behavior analytic research is disproportionately smaller and less diverse than the body of clinical targets focused on, and interventions used by, non-research oriented behavior analysts. Needed is a way to get the novel clinical perspectives out to the field at large. Publishing controlled clinical investigations is a very effective way of doing just that. And the thorough, user-friendly, and up-to-date nature of this book will make it simpler and easier for clinicians to pursue that goal. As their novel perspectives filter out to the world, the external validity of applied behavior analysis expands and the dissemination of its worldview increases.

This recommendation is not academic. I have been doing something similar for my entire career. I am not a scientist. I am a clinician, pure and simple. Over the course of that career, I have discovered some novel ways to solve clinical problems, and access to resources such as my graduate advisors and the L. Keith Miller manual have enabled me to publish small descriptions of some of these (e.g., job-based grounding, bedtime pass, alarm treatment for diurnal enuresis). Mine are not highly influential systematic lines of study like those provided by more influential members of the behavior-analytically oriented community (e.g., Bud Mace, Jim Carr, Cathleen Piazza, Dorothea Lerman, Brian Iwata, Wayne Fisher, Ray Miltenberger, Greg Hanely). They are the empirical dabblings of a busy clinician. Be that as it may, once published they become the province of the entire field, leading to their expanded use by other clinicians and increased possibility of expanded study by genuine researchers. The field would benefit tremendously if more clinicians were to match to that sample. This book is the perfect guide for showing them how to do it.

—Patrick C. Friman, Ph.D., ABPP
Boys Town

Introduction

During graduate school, I never thought I would publish research beyond my dissertation. I always wanted to be a practitioner. If you would have told me years ago that I would publish as a regular part of my professional life, I would not have believed you. There tends to be a divide between applied work and research in our field, with many behavior analysts believing they cannot do both. There are very few examples of prolific practitioner-researchers, so I think most people make this distinction early on in their career and choose one path—either academia/research or clinical practice. I know I made this distinction and chose to be a practitioner. It was not until I observed other practitioners conducting research that I realized I could do both.

My Journey as a Practitioner-Researcher

I fell into research naturally but differently than most professionals in our field do. After my postdoctoral fellowship, I took a job in the same clinic where I had done my training, with the intent to clinically support a caseload of individuals with autism with early language development. There was a strong culture of applied research in that clinic, so I began to ask very simple applied questions, to answer those questions with one or two participants using systematic experimental design, and to more fully experience the publication process.

As an example, my very first research publication was the result of a very common clinical problem I was having. As I was teaching several clients to answer intraverbal questions, I found they often echoed the last part of my instruction. So, I might say, "What's your name?" and then prompt a child to answer "Greg," to which he would respond, "What's your name—Greg." I found this problem often popped up in teaching other verbal operants as well. For example, when teaching a tact, I might say, "What is this?" and then prompt "cup," to which the child would respond, "What is this—cup." I did some reading on this topic and discovered a small body of literature focused on a procedure called cues-pause-point (McMorrow et al., 1987). The literature addressed echolalia but did not put the procedure in the context of applied verbal behavior. When I originally went to the literature, my goal was simply to use it to address my clinical issue. But as I read further, I realized I could extend the procedures to my specific clinical problem. When I fleshed out the idea and began programming for my clients, my mentor at the time casually mentioned it could make a good contribution to the literature. And it eventually did (Valentino, Shillingsburg, Conine, & Powell, 2012)!

As a second example (Valentino, Shillingsburg, & Call, 2012), one of my early clients, Penny, was a thirteen-year-old female diagnosed with Down syndrome and autism. When she came into my care, she'd had no exposure to behavior analysis. Her echoic repertoire was not strong enough for her to engage in vocal responding, so we began teaching her simple signs. She acquired many, quite quickly, particularly in mand (request) form, so we started to teach her other verbal operants. Over the course of about seven months, her echoic repertoire had grown such that we were able to discontinue sign language and focus on vocalizations as her primary communication modality. During this transition to vocal speech, we began targeting some simple intraverbal fill-ins and basic "wh" questions (e.g., "Ready, set, ___ [go]," and "What do you throw?") using echoic prompts and a transfer of stimulus control procedure. Penny's progress was slow here, much slower that her progress with other verbal operants. But we noticed something. Although not required to do so, Penny emitted motor movements independently when responding vocally. These movements typically involved about five gross motor movements, and they did not appear to correspond with specific vocal responses. For example, at times she clapped her hands when emitting the response "go" or other vocal responses, and at other times she said "go" when emitting different motor movements.

At this point, a study was born. We questioned what role Penny's history with sign language may have in acquisition of vocal intraverbal behavior. Sign language, although topographically dissimilar to spoken language, may facilitate vocal language because both response forms may be members of the same functional stimulus class. Our study focused on a comparison of echoic prompts only, echoic prompts plus modeled prompts, and a control condition (verbal discriminative stimulus [SD] only) on the acquisition of independent intraverbal responding. We used a modified alternating treatments design with a repeated A-B design across sets of stimuli. We found that adding the modeled prompt significantly facilitated acquisition of intraverbal responding. One of the many things I love about this study is that it had significant implications for our clinical recommendations for this client. When teaching intraverbals, throw in a modeled prompt! It's easy, requires very little extra training on the part of the instructor, and results in much faster acquisition for the learner.

Although it was hard work, many of those early studies got published, which provided a solid foundation and left me excited about applied research. I started to ask more questions, and with some basic knowledge of the editorial process, continued to publish applied research over the next five years while at that clinic. When I moved on to work for a different organization, I again thought that my career as a researcher would be over. It was an active decision, and I was okay to let go of that part of my professional identity, even though I enjoyed it. I took a job as a senior clinician, again overseeing a caseload and supervising aspiring behavior analysts. I was fortunate to join another organization with a culture of applied research and an established research review committee (RRC). Importantly, I found a research mentor who was very willing to provide guidance while giving me professional autonomy to explore my own research interests. I dedicated an entire chapter in this book (chapter 8) to finding a mentor, and I highly recommend your doing so as well. My research and publishing continued, and over a decade later, here I am, writing a book about how to publish as a practitioner.

Over the years, my identity as a practitioner-researcher has evolved and matured. My interests have changed, and this evolution is what has kept me motivated. When you are in a private organization, there are no pressures or requirements to publish, so you have the freedom to explore whatever interests you. Also, you can start and stop conducting research any time you choose. This way, you know that if you continue to conduct research, it is because you truly enjoy it and not because someone else is telling you that you must do it!

This book is geared toward people in a similar position—practitioners who are not required to conduct applied research, but simply want to. It addresses common barriers to conducting research and offers you strategies for contributing to the research literature, advancing your career, and making professional scholarly contributions over the course of your professional practitioner career.

Can Research Really Be "Made Easy"?

The title of this book was quite difficult to choose and, I imagine to some, is controversial. Can research really be made "easy"? Can a practitioner sum up the complexity of a discipline's research methodology in 200 some-odd pages for anyone to follow and immediately become a published author? Of course not—single-subject methodology is complex and is not to be underestimated in terms of the skill required. So, what are we doing here, then? My goal is not to train you to do all facets of research perfectly in one handbook. My goal is to teach practitioners who already have a foundation in applied behavior analysis (ABA) research methodology to think about research differently. How to utilize what you already know in a novel way that will allow you, as a practitioner, to identify questions in your applied work that can (and should) be answered in a systematic and scientific way. How to explore your interests by seeking opportunities to cultivate a new idea or propose a model for practice. These are tasks practitioners are uniquely equipped to engage in—and are likely doing so every day: good clinical practice. In this book, I hope to teach you to see those tasks from a slightly different lens and to consider the possibility that your clinical work could become contributions to the field. It is my hope that this book will get you from "I have an idea" to "I have a contribution."

The road to get from point A to point B takes persistence, focus, and acquisition of a few new skills, but in this book, I will outline how to get there. I will define the research-to-practice gap and why you should care about it, and I'll discuss why practitioners should publish (if you're not already convinced that they should). I devote two chapters to ethical research practices and a chapter to time management and staying productive. We will also discuss obstacles and barriers many practitioners face when trying to conduct research—and how to overcome them. You'll learn strategies you can implement to ensure your success, we'll explore receiving mentorship, and I'll provide tips for writing. Finally, I'll outline how the editorial process typically works and conclude with dozens of resources (organized around common topics) for you to explore on your own research journey.

I recognize that you may find yourself comparing your experience to mine and realize that you come from a different background or are presented with unique challenges that I did not face. This book is intended to address common obstacles and barriers faced by people from different clinical and educational backgrounds with a variety of experiences. Depending on your profile, certain chapters may be more meaningful than others.

Here are a few profiles of people with different backgrounds and how the book will help them. Hopefully, you can relate to at least one of them, using that profile as a guide for how to get the most out of this book.

> *Tommy is a behavior analyst practitioner with about five years of clinical work experience. His master's program provided him with a strong foundation in research methodology, and he thought he might go on to get his PhD. However, he found his way into meaningful clinical practice and never looked back. Tommy knows that he has a lot of research in him, but he does not quite know where to begin. He has a copy of Bailey and Burch's Research Methods and Applied Behavior Analysis, which is going to be his guide to research methods and experimental design. He needs help developing the research potential in his clinical practice. He needs encouragement and a reminder that his unique perspective really is valuable to the community.*

In Tommy's case, he already has a strong interest and foundation in research. He can also reference existing resources to guide the technical part of conducting research. Tommy is an experienced clinician, so he likely has established practical skills that may provide fluency to his clinical work—and that he may not have if he were fresh out of graduate school. His challenges include difficulty merging research and practice and lack of confidence necessary to know that he has something valuable to add to the behavior analytic literature.

If you find yourself in the same boat as Tommy, this book is for you. Chapter 2 will be immensely helpful in boosting your confidence. It talks about why ABA practitioners should publish and the unique valuable perspective practitioners can bring to the table. Chapter 7, on practical strategies, will also be useful; this chapter outlines some ways you can think about research that you may not have considered. For example, aside from direct data collection with participants, there are other ways to contribute to the research, such as conducting literature reviews or writing papers on recommended practice guidelines. These other research areas may help stimulate ideas you had not fully considered before. Finally, reading chapter 8 on mentorship will be helpful. A mentor could support you in your first project by providing guidance on asking applied questions and giving you the confidence needed to see a study through to the end.

> *Porter is a board-certified behavior analyst (BCBA), one year post graduate school. He did not receive a strong foundation in research methods in his graduate program. He is very interested in research but does not feel he has the skills to act upon this interest. He has a lot of good ideas but is not sure how to structure his research study ideas properly. He needs help choosing an experimental design, asking the right research questions, and engaging in visual inspection of his data.*

Porter feels he needs a stronger foundation in research methodology. If you are in this boat, I encourage you to challenge that feeling a bit. While you may not feel fully confident, you are likely more equipped than you think you are. Every program in behavior analysis has experimental design and research methodology as a requirement, so you may want to review your textbook notes in this area. While this book will not teach you experimental design, it can still be helpful in several ways. Utilize the recommendations in chapter 8 on mentorship and try to identify a mentor with strong research methodology skills—ideally one who uses those skills when conducting applied research. Additionally, review the sample studies throughout the text, as these will give you ideas of how studies are designed so you can imitate some of that good research methodology. When I started conducting research, this is exactly what I did—I looked at applied studies and used similar setups for my research. As I got more experienced, I deviated from the models, but when starting out there is nothing wrong with replicating the design and arrangement of a similar study.

> *Avelyn is a BCBA who has been in the field for ten years. She feels great about her research skills and even presented at a few conferences early in her career. She continuously thinks about and asks applied research questions in her work. Avelyn is motivated, but she often finds it difficult to prioritize her research. Every time she gets started, she loses focus, switches tasks, and starts prioritizing other things. Avelyn really wants to contribute to the literature but needs help organizing and managing her time.*

If you find yourself relating to Avelyn, there are several parts of this book to focus on. Chapter 5 is entirely dedicated to time management and staying productive. Avelyn is motivated and experienced and has good ideas. However, time management can really be a source of stress for her. In chapter 7, I'll provide specific strategies to help you overcome the competing contingencies unique to clinical work and create actionable items to begin prioritizing research as part of your everyday life.

> *Sawyer is a new BCBA who just started his first job as a clinician at a large organization. He was a very strong student, graduating at the top of his class and feeling confident in the material he learned. However, after he joined the organization, he began to identify gaps in his knowledge and started to lose his confidence. He intended to conduct applied research in his new role—in fact, the organization already had an infrastructure to support this. However, after working for a few weeks, he became fearful of taking the next step in research, questioning his abilities. He thought he might make a mistake, so he avoided approaching anyone about it at all. He stuck to his role as a practitioner, but he has a nagging feeling that he is missing a great opportunity and not cultivating his practice as much as he could be by exploring applied research questions.*

Sawyer is lucky to have joined an organization with an established research culture. As he navigates his new role, he will need to acquire new clinical skills and apply the theoretical work he learned in graduate school. If you can relate to Sawyer's situation, several parts of this book will be helpful. Chapter 6 includes a section on overcoming fears, a very common barrier acknowledged by BCBA clinicians. One of the important things to do when you are fearful is to expose yourself to the situation. So, reading this book is a great start. Use it as a guide to get started on your research journey, and do not avoid diving in—having the experiences (and being okay with making mistakes) will help you overcome the fear you feel about pursuing your interests.

> Jordan is a Board Certified Behavior Analyst - Doctoral (BCBA-D) and the clinical director of a midsize provider that serves children with autism. She has been in the field for about seven years. Like Sawyer, her organization provides support for research, has its own RRC, and even provides some funding for conference attendance for those interested in presenting. On the surface, Jordan has always said she wants to do research. She's had a few good ideas and often reads behavior analytic articles to help guide her clinical work. She can't quite put her finger on why, but she just cannot seem to get started on incorporating research into her practice.

If you are like Jordan, you may find that you have a motivational issue. This can be difficult to piece apart from a skill deficit, so I spend much of chapter 5 discussing how to tell the difference between the two and what to do to increase motivation. While that chapter will be particularly helpful, the book in its entirety will too, inspiring you to contribute in a way that only you are uniquely equipped to do.

> Hazel loved conducting her master's thesis. In fact, she even collected more participants than were required and submitted her thesis for publication, even though this was not required. To her surprise, her thesis got accepted for publication into a peer-reviewed behavior analytic journal. She joined a very small organization, owned by a well-known BCBA who had published early in her career. Hazel spoke to the owner herself during the interview process, expressing her desire to conduct research. The owner assured her there would be opportunity to do so, and Hazel chose to work for this organization for that reason. Hazel has now been working for that company for nine months, and despite trying to organize studies and talking to the owner about research, she has not made any progress. There just are not any opportunities. Hazel wonders if she is taking the right approach to trying to get things started. She thinks the owner will be receptive to her ideas, but she hasn't figured out the specific actions that will motivate the owner to create these research opportunities.

If you are in a situation like Hazel's, it is a pretty good place to be. There are lots of ideas in this book, particularly in chapter 7, about how you can create your own opportunities, establish a research community, and pursue ideas. Hazel just doesn't have the right tools to get her started or specific actionable items to pursue to put her on a path to success.

Below, you'll find a summary of each of these fictional character's strengths, their barriers to conducting research, and which chapters in the book will be most valuable. Consider your own barriers, and use this chart to create your own action list.

Character	Strengths	Barriers	Focus on
Tommy	Strong interest Solid research foundation Experienced clinician	Merging research into practice Lack of confidence	Chapters 2, 7, and 8
Porter	Strong interest Good ideas	Strong research methods foundation	Chapter 8
Avelyn	Good ideas Research experience Motivated Experienced clinician	Time management	Chapters 5 and 7
Sawyer	Strong conceptual skills Organizational support	Fear	Chapter 7
Jordan	Organizational support Good ideas In touch with the literature	Motivational deficit	Chapter 5
Hazel	Publication history Motivated	No opportunities	Chapter 7

I hope you can relate to one of these fictional people (or maybe a combination of a few of them). If so, use that as guidance for areas to focus on and to gain a deeper understanding of your commitment to a professional path of applied research.

How to Get the Most out of This Book

You will find that this book is written in a very informal, casual tone, which is intentional. It is my strong desire to make research approachable—something that feels consistent with the work you do every day as a practitioner, not something far reaching and overly difficult. My experience as an applied researcher will offer valuable insight to get you started on a similar path. I offer many strategies that can help you be productive and stay focused. I think you will find that you are closer to conducting research than you may have thought—indeed, you do much of it every day in your clinical work. Here are my recommendations for getting the most out of this book:

Read the chapters in order, at least for the first read through. It may be tempting to skip ahead or only focus on certain chapters. However, the chapters are ordered in a way that should guide you along a focused path toward research.

The book is full of worksheets, questions, and reflection activities, some of which are also available to download at the website for this book, http://www.newharbinger.com/47827. (See the very back of this book for more details.) Do those exercises when you come to them in the book. The text preceding the exercises will help stimulate your thoughts about those activities so you get the most out of them. While you may want to come back and revisit your responses to some of the questions over time, filling them in when you are most prepared to do so will set you up to be successful.

Commit to reading the book within a certain time frame, but do not cram it all in during one session. Make reading this book and completing the corresponding activities the first thing on your research to-do list. A few chapters a day with some days in between is ideal. On the days that you don't read, reflect on your motivation and your plan and jot down any ideas that come up. When you've completed the entire book, summarize what you've learned, reflect on it, and begin implementing your new research plan. If you follow this general timeline, you could finish the book in its entirety over the span of three to four weeks. I do not recommend taking more than two days off in a row, as you might lose momentum and forget the material you read.

After reading this book, it is my sincere hope that you'll have the necessary tools to take your desire to become an applied researcher to the next step through presenting and publishing. Happy reading!

CHAPTER 1

The Research-to-Practice Gap

The research-to-practice gap is exactly what it sounds like—a disconnect that exists due to missing information between the evidence base in a field and how people practice. The research-to-practice gap can be bidirectional, consisting of practitioners failing to implement research findings or researchers failing to investigate relevant clinical areas of concern (Valentino & Juanico, 2020). This gap has been cited as a common occurrence in many disciplines, such as human resources (Rynes et al., 2002) and psychology (Wandersman et al., 2008). As an example, a field might rely heavily on a type of assessment or test prior to its being evaluated as an effective tool for predicting a certain behavior or set of behaviors.

There have been no formal studies investigating (or trying to bridge) the research-to-practice gap in the field of applied behavior analysis (ABA), but I hypothesize that it exists in both directions. I am sure you can recall a time when you or a peer implemented a procedure and later learned that there was a newer way to implement that intervention based on recent research findings. For example, perhaps you tried a unique prompting strategy to teach vocalizations or modified a treatment protocol for problem behavior that consisted of a different component than is commonly used to treat that issue. You have also likely read a research article and wondered how it applies to your clinical work. For example, perhaps you read an article on a training procedure involving many steps that are very difficult to implement in practice and contemplated how you might use that procedure in your own practice.

In a unique study, Kelley et al. (2015) identified prolific practitioner-researchers in behavior analysis and interviewed them to create a list of recommendations for practitioners wanting to conduct research in clinical practice. Kelley et al.'s research was initiated because they noticed the research-to-practice gap and attributed that gap to a large increase in demand for services, resulting in an increase in the number of practitioners certified as BCBAs while the number of researchers in academic settings producing studies has remained very low. They wanted to publish work that encouraged practitioners to conduct more research during applied practice to be sure publications remain steady, despite the gap between the number of practitioners and researchers.

Problems Created by the Gap

If many disciplines have a gap between research and practice, you might be asking yourself why you should care and why behavior analysts should work to resolve it. Two main problems occur when a research-to-practice gap exists. First, the gap can lead to practitioners engaging in out-of-date practices, and second, the reverse: the gap can lead to researchers conducting research that is not informed by applied issues.

Let's talk first about practitioners engaging in out-of-date practices, which may lead to lack of progress for ABA consumers. As an example, historically, practitioners implemented receptive language training using mass trials and did not commonly implement conditional discrimination training. The literature on this topic has evolved over time, and while still in early stages, research suggests that receptive language training should occur with larger arrays and very specific conditional discrimination training (Green, 2001; Grow & LeBlanc, 2013). As another example, you have likely implemented an analogue functional analysis (FA; Iwata et al., 1982/1994) to determine the function of a behavior and develop a function-based treatment. Over time, this technology has evolved and changed the way we practice. For example, a variety of different FA types are now available to choose from based on the consumer's profile, obstacles, and intended intervention (Iwata & Dozier, 2008). Finally, recent research has proposed even more options, such as a synthesized functional analysis (Jessel et al., 2016). This type of evolution has occurred in so many areas—we now have different types of preference assessments (Heinicke et al., 2016) and are much more sophisticated in the way we teach mands for information under appropriate stimulus control (e.g., Shillingsburg et al., 2014; Valentino et al., 2019).

Take a few moments to think about literature you have read that changed the way you practiced. Jot those articles down, along with how they changed your clinical approach. This exercise will help you focus on the importance of keeping up to date on the research literature and allowing it to inform your practice.

_____

_____

_____

_____

_____

As I'm sure you know, it's extremely important to keep up to date on the literature to implement best practice. However, the reverse is also true—it's important to ask applied research questions to influence the unresolved questions that remain in your clinical work and in our field. Not doing so constitutes the second problem that can occur as a result of the research-to-practice gap: that the literature does not grow quickly and cannot keep up with the applied issues that are real and meaningful for those who practice. Although much of the literature has indeed evolved out of applied questions, it's not enough—there are hundreds if not thousands of applied questions that have yet to be asked (and answered). And, practitioners are the ones who can and should be answering them!

How to Help Bridge the Gap

The solution to bridging the gap may seem obvious. If you are a practitioner reading this book, the solution is to start conducting applied research. This will help bridge the gap in both directions—you will become more familiar with the literature as a result of your own research endeavors, and you will ask and answer applied questions to inform the field. I encourage practitioners to commit to conducting some form of applied research over the course of their career. However, even if half of the practitioners contributed one piece of work, we would be in a much better position as a field. So, exactly how do you go about committing to a research path in your own career? As an overview, you will need to take several steps, which this book outlines in detail:

- Decide what to research.

- Identify the reasons you want to conduct research, including consideration of benefits to both the field and you.

- Ensure that you follow ethical research practices.

- Arrange for optimal use of your time and for a plan to stay productive.

- Identify your barriers and obstacles—and establish a plan to overcome them.

- Implement practical strategies to make research approachable and integrated into your practice.

- Identify a mentor.

- Write!

- Understand the editorial process and begin to take part in it.

What to Research

Prior to reading this book, you might have already been convinced that you should conduct research and should be interested in doing so. However, narrowing down a research question or even topic may prove difficult. Finding an area to research is a combination of interest paired with convenience and opportunity. Additionally, the exact question must not have already been answered in the literature (unless you are looking to do an exact replication study, which is a great area to focus on in most cases!). These elements must come together or you are unlikely to be successful. For example, you might be interested in researching a topic in verbal behavior with young children with autism. If you are employed at a residential facility for adults with intellectual disability, you will not have the opportunity to explore this research interest. Equally so, if you are completely uninterested in research questions that involve the population with whom you work, you will likely burn out quickly and lose interest in your work. Choosing a topic is a very personal decision. Here is a simple flowchart that can help you narrow down a possible research topic.

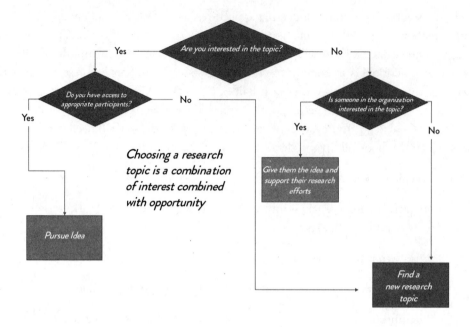

Below are the questions on the flowchart. You can fill in your responses here.

Are you interested in the topic? (Here, you might also write a bit about why you are or are not interested.)

- _____

_____

_____

- _____

_____

_____

- _____

_____

_____

- _____

_____

_____

Do you have access to appropriate participants (if participants are required)?

- _____

_____

_____

- _____

_____

_____

- _____

_____

_____

- _____

_____

_____

Is someone in the organization interested in the topic?

- _____

_____

_____

- _____

_____

_____

- _____

_____

_____

Here are some examples of how I might answer these questions.

Are you interested in the topic?

- *Yes, I am interested in verbal behavior research in young children with autism. This is how I got started in the field of ABA, and as I've learned more about applied verbal behavior, I find myself asking many questions about how to best teach certain operants.*

- *Yes, I am interested in effective staff training procedures. I have found that my organization often relies heavily on verbal instruction, and this typically does not result in team members competently performing different parts of their job. I know there is a large body of staff training literature, so I have a lot to learn but think there could be opportunity to do some research while solving some of the training issues within my organization.*

- *No, I am not interested in verbal behavior research. Although much of my job focuses on children with autism and teaching verbal behavior, I think I only considered it because of convenience, not interest. I am excited about other topics, like professional practice issues (e.g., supervision, ethics).*

Do you have access to appropriate participants (if participants are required)?

- *Yes! The category of verbal behavior research applies to most of my clients, and I could very easily ask applied questions during my clinical work with them.*

- *Yes! I work in a hospital setting alongside nutritionists, and I support people in making healthy lifestyle choices. I am very interested in obesity research and think there could be an avenue to utilize behavior analytic procedures with this population more fully while conducting research on the topic.*

- *No—most of my clients are adults with intellectual disability. I would need to work with another organization or practitioner to fully accomplish these research goals. This does not seem feasible currently.*

Is someone in the organization interested in the topic?

- *Yes, there is a new clinician in my organization who is very passionate about verbal behavior research. Although it is not an interest of mine, I could work with her to pursue the topic and support her in her research endeavors.*

- *Yes, a graduate student who has almost completed her PhD is very interested in this topic. I could support her development by allowing her to take the lead.*

- *No, there is not anyone interested in this topic. It may be time to move on to something else.*

Most of my applied research studies were generated exactly this way—through my discovering a practical issue that did not have any literature to support me through it. So, I or my colleagues created the study, asked the question, and answered it. Here are examples of some of the clinical issues we came up with over the course of our research careers that eventually led to research questions and studies, many which were published:

- I struggle with the fact that many children on my caseload echo the SD and the vocal prompt when I teach them intraverbal language. I am not sure what to do about this issue. I've tried basic prompting strategies and differential reinforcement, but nothing seems to be working.

- I have a client who elopes. I have a good intervention in place, but it requires 100 percent integrity with blocking. I know his caregivers cannot block his elopement all the time. I wonder if it would be effective if they did not block every time. How much is enough to maintain the treatment effects?

- I really want to teach several clients on my caseload to ask the question "why," but it is a little difficult to establish correctly. I can teach them to ask the question "why" to receive an edible item, but that isn't how people ask this question in real language. How can I teach that behavior (a mand for information) under appropriate motivational control so that it sounds natural and occurs naturally?

- I'd like to teach children to discriminate across motivating operations when asking "wh" questions. I played around with a strategy that might be effective, but I need a more structured process to evaluate it.

- I am interested in implementing best practices in supervision, but I can't seem to find any guidance in the behavior analytic literature. I have some good ideas and things that have worked well with my supervisees, and I know several colleagues who also seem to have very effective supervision practices. I wonder if there might be an opportunity to write those up and share them with the field.

- Group supervision seems to be interpreted differently across the field. I have talked with other colleagues who think about group supervision differently than I do. I wonder if there is an opportunity to more clearly define these strategies and make some recommendations to the field about how to utilize a group to optimize the benefits of that structure. To my knowledge, no literature of this kind exists already, so it could make a great contribution.

- I have always struggled with the decision of which alternative communication system to use, especially when deciding between pictures and sign language. It would be great if there were a prerequisite assessment that I could give to assess which modality a child would do best in. I have some ideas about what prerequisite skills might be associated with success in each. Perhaps I could develop a brief assessment and assess its efficacy in predicting success in sign language and picture systems.

- I have a client who eats very rapidly, and we are concerned about risks associated with this behavior, including choking and difficulty fitting in during social meals. I need an easy and discreet way to reduce his pace of eating.

- I have several clients on my caseload who are struggling to learn motor imitation when an object is not involved. No matter how hard I try and what reinforcer I use, I can't establish this skill. I need an intervention to address any deficits my clients might be facing that would help them learn gross motor imitation. I have some ideas about those deficits and ways I could ameliorate them. I wonder if addressing them could improve performance in this area.

- One of my clients is ready for very advanced intraverbal language—telling a story after it has been read to him. I've never taught this skill before, and I'm not sure if standard prompting procedures (e.g., vocal prompts) will work. I have used text prompts with him and utilized some slow fading; I could turn that into a structured protocol and evaluate its effectiveness.

- A client on my caseload engages in unique behavior—she makes up her own models when responding vocally to simple intraverbal questions. She is new to vocalizing. I wonder if I could design a procedure to utilize a modeled prompt to see if that facilitates faster acquisition of her intraverbal behavior.

- I have a client who is a very strong signer and asks for things he wants with sign language very consistently. During one session, I accidentally did not immediately provide the preferred item he signed for. He got a little frustrated and eventually let out a sound. He had never vocalized before, and I was very impressed with the way it sounded. Perhaps I could conceptualize this procedure in a way that utilizes extinction of the signed mand to induce vocalizations. I wonder if it would work to establish vocalizations in my learners who do not yet vocalize.

- I have a very unique case: a thirty-year-old male with autism who stopped walking about two years ago. There is no medical reason for this, and it needs to be treated behaviorally. Even if the intervention is simple, this could make a very interesting case study given the unique profile of the client.

Now I want you to spend some time noting any practical issues you've seen pop up in your clinical work that you have not found literature to guide you with. I am sure there are several. Take some time to list and describe them here. Perhaps one of these could become a research topic you pursue.

Recent research my colleague and I conducted (Valentino & Juanico, 2020) confirms that practitioners are motivated to conduct research during practice and to help bridge the research-to-practice gap. So why isn't more practitioner-led research occurring? There are several barriers and obstacles impeding practitioners from conducting research, and this book is meant to help individuals overcome many of them.

Take a few moments to identify some obstacles or barriers that you are facing in your efforts to conduct applied research.

What are those obstacles or barriers?

_____

_____

Have you attempted to overcome them?

_____

_____

What worked and what did not?

_____

_____

Here is an example of how I might answer the above questions:

Time is a big barrier for me. Since my organization does not pay me to do research, I must see a certain number of clients and conduct applied clinical work every day. My schedule is full. I have some time in the early mornings and evenings, but I feel so overwhelmed by even starting to think about research that I often give up. I've tried taking some initial steps on the weekends but still feel overwhelmed by the task at hand, even though I am excited to start conducting research.

It is my sincere hope that practitioners wishing to conduct applied research will use this book as a resource and source of motivation to begin doing so. I also hope that as a behavior analytic community, we work more to support practitioners in their research endeavors. Organizations that employ behavior analysts should consider ways to allow opportunities for research, and senior leaders in our field should determine ways to mentor and support practitioners. More partnerships and close coordination between practitioners and academics should occur pertaining to practical issues in the field that should be investigated. Our field will greatly benefit from these contributions in the form of answers to applied questions, a more research-engaged and connected practitioner group, and overall long-term career satisfaction. Importantly, these efforts are likely to bridge the research-to-practice gap that exists in our field.

Essential Takeaways

The research-to-practice gap is real, and there are several barriers and obstacles associated with closing it. Right now, just focus on considering the obstacles and barriers *you* face. We'll discuss what to do about them in future chapters. The important work to do at this point is to identify what you're up against. You may have never sat down to consider these obstacles and barriers before, and simply doing so will start you on a journey to take action to overcome any challenges you might be facing. Before we get into the precise actions, let's talk next about why ABA practitioners should publish.

CHAPTER 2

Why ABA Practitioners Should Publish

Since you are reading this book, you likely have an interest in publishing but may not be convinced yet that you should publish, or you may not understand all the benefits of doing so. You might find yourself in a similar situation to Tommy, having a strong interest and foundation in research, but having difficulty merging research into practice and lacking confidence in your ability to do so. Or, perhaps you are like Porter, also having the interest but lacking a strong foundation in research methodology. You might also be struggling with time management, motivational issues, or fear, or you might simply not have any opportunities. With all these obstacles and barriers, it is natural to ask, why should ABA practitioners even try to publish? In short, there are several benefits to the field, to you as a practitioner-researcher, and to you personally. I want to explore each of these to widen your perspective on the importance of practitioners contributing to the field through applied research.

Benefits to the Field

Benefits to the field include advancement, making a unique and individual contribution, helping consumers and the general public, helping other researchers, and serving as a role model for other practitioners. Let's explore each of these in detail.

Field Advancement

First, research advances our field. There are so many unanswered questions—and every study, big or small, contributes to our knowledge and answers at least one of them. Even if you publish only one research study, that study will advance the field. Consider the work done in the area of problem behavior—the creation and evolution of functional analysis, which has molded how we assess and treat problem behavior. Likewise, the work done on teaching children with autism to vocalize through stimulus-stimulus pairing procedures—this work has provided direction that did not exist for that population of individuals who may not have vocalized without that new behavioral technology.

Someone will likely build upon your work, creating advancement that would not exist had you not conducted that research. For example, you might choose to conduct a study evaluating two different prompting strategies to teach a tact repertoire. In your study, you identify a third procedure, mixed prompting, that could be effective, but you did not design your study to evaluate this third method. Another researcher may read your study and decide to replicate it, adding in that third method. Or, you might even attempt to conduct that study yourself. There are dozens of examples of this in the applied literature, and one seemingly small study can be the impetus for many more studies on that topic. More and more people are seeking ABA services, so we must continue to evolve at a rapid pace in order to prevent stagnation. Our discipline has grown tremendously, and if every practitioner contributes something over the course of their career, we will have grown the literature base exponentially.

When considering how your unique contribution can advance the field, ask and answer the following questions:

1. What areas do you struggle with clinically? Do any of them have an answer in the literature?

    _____

    _____

    _____

2. If those areas do not have any literature, could you design something?

    _____

    _____

    _____

3. If they do have an answer in the literature, has that answer been helpful for all your clients? For some of them?

    _____

    _____

    _____

4. If only effective for some of your clients, what is the remaining need? Do those clients present differently? If so, how?

    _____

    _____

    _____

5. Can you identify a clinical problem that your colleagues commonly ask? A consistent pattern of deficit across caseloads?

_____

_____

_____

As you answer these and similar questions, you will begin to identify ways you can advance the field through your research. Here is an example of how I might answer the above questions, leading me toward a line of research.*

1. What areas do you struggle with clinically? Do any of them have an answer in the literature?

    I have several clients on my caseload who need help learning menstrual care skills. The literature has very dated articles that haven't been that helpful.

2. If those areas do not have any literature, could you design something?

    There are partial answers in the literature. I could look at expansion of the literature to my specific client base.

3. If they do have an answer in the literature, has that answer been helpful for all your clients? For some of them?

    The literature I found is not that helpful because it is very old and based on old menstrual-care practices and products. It was also conducted with adults in residential facilities, so it has little application to my client base.

4. If only effective for some of your clients, what is the remaining need? Do those clients present differently? If so, how?

    My clients are adolescents at home with their parents, experiencing their menstrual cycle for the first time.

5. Can you identify a clinical problem that your colleagues commonly ask? A consistent pattern of deficit across caseloads?

    Many of my colleagues have asked about how to teach menstrual-care skills and I think the need for this type of research is far reaching.

---

*   This example is based on a study conducted by Sarah Veazey (2016), the primary researcher of a study that was eventually published in *Behavior Analysis in Practice*. She worked on these questions as a part of her clinical work and engaged the help of colleagues Adeline Low and Alyssa McElroy to conduct this research. I use this as a very applied example of how someone might answer these questions, but all credit goes to Sarah and her team for actually doing this work!

As you can see, the answers to these questions would lead you toward conducting research on updated practices for teaching menstrual-care skills to adolescents with developmental disabilities in a home setting, guided by their parents. You could, of course, repeat the above exercise multiple times and identify several lines of research that would make great contributions to the field.

Unique and Individual Contribution

A lot of excitement comes with making your own unique and individual contribution to the field. Particularly if you have chosen a topic you are passionate about, the ability for you and others to see your name attached to that contribution is a purely joyful experience. Additionally, most other people will know and appreciate the hard work it takes to contribute in this way—so your unique and individual contribution will not go unnoticed. I will never forget the first time someone recognized me for a research publication at a conference; she was a student and had read one of my early articles as part of a class. I felt like a movie star—she even asked to take a selfie with me. This could happen for you, too, even when your publication history is short. Our field is small, and it consists of several even smaller special interest groups—verbal behavior, organizational behavior management, problem behavior to name a few. It is not uncommon for an article to become known as the "Smith article," identifiable by its first author. When you publish in a specific area, you make an impact, one that will be acknowledged by the behavior analytic community.

To support development of your own unique and individual contribution, spend some time asking and answering the following questions:

1. What am I passionate about?

   _____

   _____

   _____

2. Is there an area of literature that has a big gap, one which I could contribute to and become known for?

   _____

   _____

   _____

3. Could I present on this topic confidently and with excitement?

_____

_____

_____

4. Do I have knowledge of the topic already or could I quickly gain that knowledge to begin making a contribution?

_____

_____

_____

Here is a sample of how you might answer those questions, leading to development of your unique ideas that will contribute to the field.

1. What am I passionate about?

   I am very excited about professional practice issues such as ethics and supervision. I find myself thinking of ways to improve these areas in my own organization. I've outlined several policies and processes to support development of these areas.

2. Is there an area of literature that has a big gap, one which I could contribute to and become known for?

   The supervision literature seems to be lacking in some areas. Although I've seen an increase in this body of literature in the past few years, there are very few data-based studies and many unanswered questions.

3. Could I present on this topic confidently and with excitement?

   Absolutely. I love talking about supervision and teaching people new things to consider. I even presented a journal club at the company I work for about a supervision article—it was a ton of fun!

4. Do I have knowledge of the topic already or could I quickly gain that knowledge to begin making a contribution?

   I have stayed connected to the literature on this topic to help guide my own clinical supervision efforts. I feel knowledgeable and have several ideas I could execute soon.

Helps Consumers and the General Public

There is no doubt that contributing to the literature helps the general public, not just a specific population. Behavior analysts have influenced many areas in the general population, such as effective toilet training methods for typically developing children (Azrin & Foxx, 1971), sleep habits (Jin & Hanley, 2013), and establishing varied eating behaviors (Rivas et al., 2014). When you publish, you create a permanent and tangible document that anyone can access. In situations where behavior analysis makes it to mainstream media, this impact is magnified. And even if your personal article is not referenced, it is one piece of literature that likely contributed to the research that does get more broadly cited—and that is important!

On a smaller scale, your research article will have greatly and positively impacted the individual participants in your study. You will have identified a procedure that could address a specific need and used that procedure to effectively address that issue.

As an example of this, my colleagues and I published a case study in the *Journal of Applied Behavior Analysis* a few years ago (Valentino et al., 2018). The participant in the study, Mason, was a ten-year-old male diagnosed with autism. He was referred to us for treatment of his very fast pace of eating. When he was younger, he engaged in food selectivity that was successfully treated by a behavior analyst—fast-forward many years later and we have a ten-year-old boy with the opposite problem now. I conducted some observations in the home, and his pace was very obviously different from that of his family. Many of his extended family members lived close by, so it was not at all uncommon for there to be big meals with family members congregating, socializing, and eating at a normal pace. Mason would come in, grab his food, scarf it down, and not have the opportunity to participate in these family events. Plus, his mom was concerned about weight gain and potential choking. An interesting addition is that his mom was very insistent that we not use physical prompts—not because she didn't want us to touch him but because he could slow his pace when physically guided (they had done a lot of this), and she wanted to fade those prompts and have him eat independently.

When we looked at the literature, we found that vibrating pagers had been used to successfully prompt individuals with autism to engage in socially significant behaviors such as social initiations (Shabani et al., 2002), language (Taylor & Levin, 1998), and seeking assistance when lost (Taylor et al., 2004). Additionally, Anglesea et al. (2008) successfully utilized a vibrating pager to slow the pace of food consumption for three adolescents with autism who had a history of rapid eating. An interesting component of this body of literature is the lack of good strategies for fading these tactile prompts. For example, Taylor and Levin (1998) evaluated whether a remote-activated vibrating pager could be used to increase the language of a child with autism. The pager prompt was effective in establishing the language target, but there were no attempts to fade the prompts. Shabani et al. (2002) replicated the beneficial effects of pager prompts for teaching social initiations to children with autism and attempted to fade the prompts by altering the schedule of prompt delivery (i.e., prompt less frequently). This fading strategy was ineffective—the children did not maintain social initiations and responses at the desired level once the pager was removed.

Given these earlier findings, with Mason, we (Valentino et al., 2018) replicated the procedures used by Anglesea et al. (2008) to slow the pace of food consumption and extended that research in two ways. The first extension was to examine whether the pager prompt could be successfully faded by altering the intensity of the vibration. The second was to compare the effects of fading by stimulus intensity vs. fading by stimulus frequency. The third author's father developed a special pager that allowed manipulation of the intensity of vibration. We determined Mason's pace of eating was about twice as fast as that of a typical adult male, and we were able to utilize the pager prompt to slow his pace to an appropriate level.

This intervention had such a positive impact on Mason. The risks associated with his fast pace of eating were gone and he was able to participate in his family mealtime more fully and with ease. His parents were thrilled with the results, and we learned a lot about how to teach him other skills and how to effectively fade our prompts. This type of very real and close connection is possible for you as a researcher, and you will undoubtedly realize your contribution to the individual participants when you are finished with the study!

To help you think through how your research can help consumers and the general public, spend some time asking and answering the following questions:

1. Is there something one or more of my clients are struggling with?

   _____

   _____

   _____

   _____

2. Is it an area I hear others express concerns about?

   _____

   _____

   _____

   _____

3. Are these concerns specific to a certain population or are they applicable to the general public?

   _____

   _____

   _____

   _____

4. If I were to identify an effective procedure, how might it help my client? Other clients? The general public?

_____

_____

_____

_____

Here is how I might have answered those questions for my study with Mason:

1. Is there a task that one or more of my clients is struggling with?

    Yes—one of my clients is struggling with pace of eating. He eats much too quickly, and his parents are concerned about it. I have another client who has the opposite problem—he eats too slowly. Perhaps I can come up with something to address both issues.

2. Is it an area I hear others express concerns about?

    Yes, a graduate school friend of mine mentioned that several of the clients on her caseload also engaged in a pace of eating that is too fast. She was unsure how to address this issue.

3. Are these concerns specific to a certain population or are they applicable to the general public?

    Although I am not fully in touch with other populations, I imagine that many children with and without disabilities also struggle with eating too fast. I often hear parents tell their children to slow down when eating. My son often eats too fast and does not always respond to my verbal instruction to slow down.

4. If I were to identify an effective procedure, how might it help my client? Other clients? The general public?

    It is possible that the procedure I identify to help my clients slow their pace of eating could also be used to address other similar concerns, such as speaking too quickly or failing to engage in social interaction at an appropriate pace. This could support the progress of other individuals in these areas as well, including those without disabilities. When designing my study, I should consider procedures that are socially acceptable and sustainable by natural care providers without a background in behavior analysis. I should consider a wide range of skill sets for which my intervention could be applicable.

I want to end with a personal experience that highlights the contribution to the general population that your research can make. Approximately five years ago, I was at a professional conference and a woman approached me. She asked if I was Amber Valentino, and when I replied yes, she went on to explain that she was the mother of a seven-year-old child with autism. She had read a study that I published about a year prior regarding a procedure used to establish vocalizations, and she had successfully used that procedure to help her child do the same. Until that time, it was not fully apparent to me that anyone (including parents of kids with autism) could (or would) access my research and use it to help them. Of course, I knew it was possible, but I had never met someone who did so, so the idea seemed very distant and abstract. Every now and again, a practitioner, another researcher, or a consumer will contact me and state the same thing. If I had to choose the one driver for me to continue publishing, this would be it. When I practice, I absolutely influence the consumers I serve. I also influence the consumers of my supervisees and, in my current role, the consumers in an entire company. However, when I add publishing to my professional career, the number of consumers who could be influenced by that research grows significantly. Focusing on this contribution is likely to motivate you too—as positively influencing the lives of others is likely what got you into the field of ABA in the first place.

Helps Other Researchers

Your contributions also help other researchers. Often, when I need a research idea or am struggling to move along with a project, I read literature on the same topic. The discussion sections of articles are filled with ideas of what remains unanswered and the limitations of the current research to be overcome in future studies (many of which the authors of the article may never explore). These ideas help other researchers immensely! As an example, for the pace of eating study with Mason that I referenced earlier in this chapter—I read research on the tactile prompt literature, specifically on pace of eating. The article I ultimately published in the *Journal of Applied Behavior Analysis* was an extension of the literature I found on tactile prompts and specifically furthered Anglesea et al.'s 2008 study. Although I will often publish several studies in one line of research, there have been times in my career when I've only published one study on a topic. For example, the study on the cues-pause-point procedure to address echolalia (Valentino, Shillingsburg, Conine, & Powell, 2012) was a one-time deal—but other researchers extended that body of literature, specifically building on my work (Kodak et al., 2013). Inevitably, another researcher will run with the idea and continue that line of study. It is thrilling to see that you started a wave of ideas that others will continue to build upon for years to come!

Here are some questions to ask and answer when considering how your work can help other researchers:

1. Have I read an idea in another article that might serve as a foundation for my work?

   _____

   _____

   _____

   _____

2.   Could I help push a body of literature along by contributing to it? If so, how?

_____

_____

_____

_____

3.   Do I think my research idea will generate other ideas (or has it already)? If so, what are they?

_____

_____

_____

_____

Here is how I might answer those questions, related to the cues-pause-point study referenced above.

1.   Have I read an idea in another article that might serve as a foundation for your work?

Yes, I read about the cues-pause-point procedure in the Journal of Applied Behavior Analysis. However, that procedure was not placed in the context of applied verbal behavior, and no other articles have been published on the topic since the mid-1980s.

2.   Could I help push a body of literature along by contributing to it? If so, how?

I could apply the technique to a common modern clinical problem and set it in the context of applied verbal behavior. I think this would offer a solution to a common clinical problem and reinvigorate the cues-pause-point research, which hasn't been referenced in a long time.

3.   Do I think my research idea will generate other ideas (or has it already)? If so, what are they?

I definitely think the research could generate other ideas. On a basic level, the same procedure could be applied to different verbal operants, such as tacts, intraverbals, or echoics. Someone could conduct a comparison study on the cues-pause-point procedure and other training procedures to determine which one is more effective.

Provides a Research Role Model for Other Practitioners

Simply by conducting research, you'll be growing the number of practitioners who are interested and competent in doing the same. This will, in turn, grow the number of research contributions made by practitioners in our field. Sometimes this modeling is done passively—simply by continuing to conduct research within a clinical role while others observe. For example, a junior colleague in your organization may observe as you collect data on a project and learn how you merge the clinical world and research world together. Or you may serve as a model for others by presenting your work at a conference and describing how you conducted the research in the context of your clinical role. Other times, modeling is done more actively—by choosing to mentor people or teach others. For example, you might form a formal mentoring relationship with a junior colleague (I provide more detail on mentoring in chapter 8) or organize a research group at your company with specific research-related training topics.

Here are some questions you can ask, answer, and act upon to maximize your ability to be a role model for other practitioners:

1. Are there people in my work environment who would benefit from observing me conduct applied research?

   _____

   _____

   _____

   _____

2. Are there people in my work environment who would like more formal mentoring on applied research?

   _____

   _____

   _____

3. What are three activities I can engage in within my organization to spread the word about applied research to others and be a role model to them?

   _____

   _____

   _____

   _____

4. What are three activities I can engage in within the field to spread the word about applied research to others and be a role model to them?

_____

_____

_____

_____

Here are sample responses to those questions:

1. Are there people in my work environment who would benefit from observing me conduct applied research?

    Yes, my company is made up of early career behavior analysts, all of whom have expressed an interest in conducting applied research. I know they look up to me for clinical guidance, so conducting research would provide a great model for them to do the same.

2. Are there people in my work environment who would like more formal mentoring on applied research?

    Yes, definitely! I can think of two clinicians who would really like some more formal mentoring. I have mentored them already on clinical issues, and they would love to extend that mentorship to applied research. I am still new to the research world, but I have confidence and motivation—we can learn together!

3. What are three activities I can engage in within my organization to spread the word about applied research to others and be a role model to them?

    Lead a research group, present research findings in a journal club, share data with my colleagues.

4. What are three activities I can engage in within the field to spread the word about applied research to others and be a role model to them?

    Present a poster at the upcoming regional conference, serve on a panel at the annual convention for applied research, and be sure to talk to people about my research at the conferences I attend this year.

One of the reasons I initially did not think I would ever become a researcher is because I did not have any models for practitioner-researchers in my immediate environment. In my mind, these two identities were mutually exclusive. A little while into my career, I was fortunate to meet a few mentors who served as the perfect practitioner-researcher role models— showing me that you could indeed be both an excellent practitioner and researcher at the same time. As I have grown in my own career, those I've supervised and mentored now see me as a role model for that practitioner-researcher identity. You can do the same!

Benefits to You

There are also several benefits to you personally. These include giving you an ego boost, giving you a career boost, making you a better practitioner, helping you question assumptions, having fun, and obtaining continuing education units. Let's explore each of these in detail.

Ego Boost

Although you may initially be hesitant to admit that publishing perks your ego, it is fine to do so! Seeing your name as an author in a journal article publication or a conference program book, hearing your name mentioned in another author's published work or presentation, and being recognized for your hard work can be a great ego boost! You worked hard and persisted. This is one of many benefits that can keep you motivated to continue publishing over time. However, it can be easy to overlook the significance of your contributions.

One way to remind yourself of them and to continue to experience a boost to your ego over time is to engage in some reflection on your progress and contributions. On a regular basis, ask yourself the following questions:

1. What have I accomplished in the past week? Month? Year?

   _____

   _____

   _____

2. What am I most proud of?

   _____

   _____

   _____

   _____

3. When was the last time I was recognized for my work?

   _____

   _____

   _____

   _____

4. What did I accomplish in addition to my research behavior?

    _____

    _____

    _____

    _____

5. What strengths have I gained as a result of my work?

    _____

    _____

    _____

    _____

6. What have I contributed to the field this week? Month? Year?

    _____

    _____

    _____

    _____

Here is an example of how I might answer those questions:

1. What have I accomplished in the past week? Month? Year?

    I've stayed on my research schedule every day this week, accomplishing 95% of the goals I set for myself. This month, I wrote an average of three days per week. This year, I submitted two articles for publication and one of them got accepted.

2. What am I most proud of?

    I am most proud that I have been able to maintain a full clinical caseload while adding research to my days. My clients are excelling, and I feel great about my work.

3. When was the last time I was recognized for my work?

    I attended the California Association for Behavior Analysis annual conference last winter. I went to a talk by my favorite behavior analyst, who published in verbal behavior. He cited my most recent publication in his presentation and used it as an example of an article that motivated him to publish the study he was presenting on. WOW!!

4.   What did I accomplish in addition to my research behavior?

I successfully integrated two main interventions that came out of my research into my clinical work. This was a big goal for me, and I wanted to ensure that research-practice connection was there. As a result of that integration, my clients overcame problems they had been struggling with for a long time.

5.   What strengths have I gained as a result of my work?

My time-management skills have gotten even better this year. I feel I've been able to manage a large workload in addition to my research endeavors. Of significance is that I feel more confident in my ability to choose the right experimental design and to execute it on a study. This is confidence I did not have a year ago and gained as a result of exposing myself to more research and trying things out for myself.

6.   What have I contributed to the field this week? Month? Year?

This week, I began mentoring a junior team member in my organization. This month, I continued work on two projects that I think will make a fantastic contribution to the literature when published. This year, I presented some work on supervision at a local regional conference—the presentation was very well received!

In addition to answering these questions and reflecting on them often, ask yourself if you are still motivated by the same things as when you began. If not, it is possible that some of the other benefits of conducting research (both for you professionally and for the field) may need to become more salient parts of your research endeavors.

Career Boost

Many employers will quickly recognize that publishing is not easy. So, if you've done some research and have that on your resume (even if it is still a work in progress), it can help your career. Conducting research can help you stand out among other applicants for a job or a promotion. You can highlight how keeping in touch with the literature (and contributing to it) makes you a better practitioner, which makes you a valuable employee to any organization. You can also highlight how you learned to multitask and accomplish research in the context of your professional work commitments. This shows commitment, willingness to go above and beyond, and creativity. It will show your employer that you are willing to put in hard work, particularly when you are passionate about something, and that you can think creatively about how to tackle multiple goals at once.

My Research Accomplishments

Use this worksheet to identify your research accomplishments and the unique strengths those accomplishments have given you that could be marketable to an employer. If you haven't started your research endeavors yet, simply save this worksheet for later, or fill it out hypothetically to begin thinking about these benefits. (You can also download this worksheet at http://www.newharbinger.com/47827.)

1. To date, I have published _____ articles, presented at _____ conferences, worked on _____ projects, and generated _____ novel research ideas. I accomplished these goals while maintaining a full-time clinical position that consisted of

    _____

    _____.

2. Maintaining a research agenda during my clinical career has made me a better

    _____

    _____.

3. The things I've learned due to conducting research include:

    _____

    _____

4. Here is one example of how being a researcher made me a better practitioner:

    _____

    _____

    _____

    _____

5. Here is one example of how being a researcher made me a better supervisor:

    _____

    _____

    _____

    _____

6. The unique things I have to offer your organization because of my research history include:

    _____

    _____

    _____

    _____

7. I can bring a research culture to your organization if hired. There are many benefits to doing so, including:

    _____

    _____

    _____

    _____

8. One requirement in the position you are seeking is that the candidate _____. I possess this skill and have exemplified it through

    _____

    _____

    _____ (Include research and non-research related tasks.)

9. The ways that research will positively augment your current clinical practice include:

    _____

    _____

    _____

    _____

10. I will continue to help your team develop professionally by:

    _____

    _____

    _____

    _____

Here is an example of how I might answer each of those questions:

1. To date, I have published *3* articles, presented at *5* conferences, worked on *10* projects, and generated *12* novel research ideas. I accomplished these goals while maintaining a full-time clinical position which consisted of *100 billable hours per month with 5 direct reports.*

2. Maintaining a research agenda during my clinical career has made me a better *time manager and practitioner.*

3. The things I've learned due to conducting research include: *how to maintain regular contact with the literature, how to manage my time, how to integrate research methodology into my clinical practice.*

4. Here is one example of how being a researcher made me a better practitioner:

   Early in my research career, I noticed that many of my clients were confusing "wh" questions. They would often answer "when" if I asked a "where" question and vice versa. I created a procedure that utilized modeled prompts associated with each "wh" question and then faded those prompts out. My clients acquired discrimination skills across "wh" questions. I wrote that study up for publication and continue to use the procedure in my everyday practice when I encounter this clinical problem.

5. Here is one example of how being a researcher made me a better supervisor:

   I had a new supervisee who was working toward board certification about 2 years ago. She was struggling with systematically introducing new procedures to address skill deficits. She would often introduce many treatment components at once and not know which, if any, made a difference. We reviewed experimental design and introducing one treatment element at a time. Although we didn't publish any research together, being a researcher helped me guide her in this practice and helped her best serve her clients.

6. The unique things I have to offer your organization because of my research history include:

   A broader perspective of our science and how it can be applied to everyday practice with clients, excellent time-management skills, passion for something related to my work, systematic analysis of intervention procedures, knowledge of the recent research literature related to the clients I will be serving.

7. I can bring a research culture to your organization if hired. There are many benefits to doing so, including:

   Less turnover, a more engaged staff, ability to attract new talent, mentorship opportunities, highlighting the organization as a thought leader in the field, marketing through presenting research at conferences.

8. One requirement for the position you are seeking is that the candidate *take initiative.* I possess this skill and have exemplified it through *starting a research culture at my current organization. This took initiative and hard work, but it was something I was passionate about, so I prioritized it while still meeting the needs of my role as a practitioner.*

9. The ways that research will positively augment your organization's current clinical practice include:

    Team members connected to the literature, engaged team members focused on professional development and keeping current, a positive reputation for contributing to the literature and being up to date on current research.

10. I will continue to help your team develop professionally by:

    establishing a research review committee, holding journal clubs, creating a research lab, and regularly presenting at conferences.

Makes You a Better Practitioner

There is no question that staying current with literature makes you a better practitioner. In order to conduct research, you need to have read literature, at least in your area of practice and preferably more broadly. This constant contact with our ever-evolving science will mold your practice and positively influence your clients. By conducting research, you also become a better consumer of the literature. You learn how to look for flaws in studies, you build upon existing knowledge of certain topics, and you learn how to interpret scientific procedures within the applied world. As an example, when I started writing up some of my clinical studies for publication, I immediately began looking more closely at my interobserver agreement (IOA) numbers. This was important to my clinical practice because I wanted to be sure that the data collected was indeed reflecting what occurred during my clients' sessions. Collection and analysis of IOA data is just as important in clinical practice as it is in research. There is typically a minimum threshold that studies must meet to be accepted (around 80% or above). When my percentages were not that high during clinical practice, I started wondering about the integrity with which my colleagues and I were collecting data and how clear my dependent variables were. I revised operational definitions and provided more training to the treatment team. This not only helped with my clinical research but improved my practice. As another example, any time I had more than one client participating in the same intervention, I staggered the baseline data to utilize a multiple baseline design. This allowed me to see experimental control where I hadn't before. It was a simple manipulation of timing of the introduction of the independent variable, but it helped me be more systematic in my clinical work.

Here are some questions you can ask and answer to support being a better practitioner through your research.

1.   How has my clinical practice changed for the better as a result of applied research?

      _____

      _____

      _____

2.   How can I integrate knowledge from my applied research into my practice to improve it?

      _____

      _____

      _____

3.   How can I continue to evolve as a practitioner by staying connected to research?

      _____

      _____

      _____

4.   What is one thing I can change based on my research activities?

      _____

      _____

      _____

Here is how I might answer those questions:

1.   How has my clinical practice changed for the better as a result of applied research?

      I am more systematic in my work. I utilize experimental design during times when I typically would not have done so. I control introduction of new treatment elements more regularly to determine the reason for any change observed.

2.   How can I integrate knowledge from my applied research into my practice to improve it?

      I can use my knowledge of experimental design to be more thoughtful in my clinical practice. By doing so, I will be knowledgeable of what I do to cause changes and can replicate that. Being sure that what I did is responsible for any changes that occur will help me know that I am investing in training of a procedure that is effective for my client.

3. How can I continue to evolve as a practitioner by staying connected to research?

    I can continue to stay skeptical of my assumptions and be systematic. By asking questions and answering them through the lens of research in my clinical practice I will better serve my clients.

4. What is one thing I can change based on my research activities?

    I can incorporate IOA into my interventions regularly. I can monitor my IOA percentages to be sure they are at an acceptable level and intervene if they are not.

Helps You Question Assumptions

Clinical practice can often be further ahead than research. It is not uncommon for practitioners to adopt a practice that has yet to be empirically supported. You might learn these practices in a workshop or read about them in recommended practice guideline papers. This is necessary—as we work with our consumers, we learn, adjust, and try things, many of which are quite beneficial. It could be detrimental to wait to try a new prompt or strategy until it has been investigated, as long as the prompt or strategy is based on a strong scientific foundation and carries little to no risk. However, these practices sometimes become so ingrained that practitioners have a difficult time changing or stopping them once research comes out that suggests they should do so. Conducting applied research can make you flexible—realizing that just because you did something before does not mean you have to do it now, especially if there is data to suggest you should not. I remember as a novice practitioner I was trained in a structural classification of language (receptive versus expressive). A few years later, I was introduced to a functional classification of language—verbal behavior. In order to adopt best practices in discrete trial teaching for my clients, I needed to change much of what I was doing—my philosophy, framework, teaching procedures, data sheets, language assessments, training materials, and so on. I had to learn many new skills. I may have been more resistant to doing so had I not had the experience of continuously changing, based on the newest research, before my formal applied introduction to verbal behavior.

Here are a few questions you can ask and answer yourself to be sure you use your research efforts to question assumptions about your clinical practice.

1. What have I learned through my own research that changes my clinical practice?

    _____

    _____

    _____

    _____

2. What have I learned through reading others' research that changes my clinical practice?

_____

_____

_____

_____

3. List a few common clinical practices that you can regularly examine to determine any shifts that should take place given what you learn through research.

_____

_____

_____

_____

Here are some examples of how to answer those questions:

1. What have I learned through my own research that changes my clinical practice?

I once had a strong opinion that the only alternative communication system that should be used is sign language. We conducted a study comparing sign language to picture systems and found that picture systems were acquired more quickly for some children. I should be more open to other forms of alternative communication.

2. What have I learned through reading others' research that changes my clinical practice?

In my literature search on alternative communication systems for the above study, I read an article with a unique approach to establishing vocalizations, called stimulus-stimulus pairing. I have several clients who are struggling to vocalize, and I think this procedure might work for them.

3. List a few common clinical practices that you can regularly examine to determine any shifts that should take place given what you learn through research.

Choice of alternative communication system, use of tact prompts to establish intraverbals, errorless prompting procedures, order of functional analysis conditions.

It's Fun

Though it can be intimidating, once you get the hang of the editorial process and obtain your first publication, you will be hooked! It is extremely fun to take an idea, formulate a research question, collect data, and write something that gets accepted for publication! Your reinforcers may be different and may vary over the course of your research career. For example, when I first started researching, publishing—and specifically the number of publications I had—was very important to me. Over time, those reinforcers have shifted. It is equally reinforcing to mentor someone else to get their first publication. It is also reinforcing for me to publish on specific areas of interest, such as supervision. I also greatly enjoy public speaking, so being invited to speak at a conference is very rewarding. Continue to evaluate what motivates you and steer your research efforts toward those motivators.

Here are some questions you can ask yourself to ensure you continue to have fun in your research work.

1. What about my research work motivates me most?

    _____

    _____

    _____

2. Have those motivators changed recently? If so, how?

    _____

    _____

    _____

3. What can I do to ensure I stay motivated to conduct research?

    _____

    _____

    _____

4. How often should I assess my feelings about research?

    _____

    _____

    _____

Here is how I might answer those questions:

1. What about my research work motivates me most?

    I still truly enjoy having a manuscript accepted for publication. Over the past year, I've noticed that it is also really enjoyable to have a coauthor experience the publication process for the first time.

2. Have those motivators changed recently? If so, how?

    The motivation to support others is newer to me.

3. What can I do to ensure I stay motivated to conduct research?

    I should incorporate junior colleagues into research studies more often and consider starting a mentoring program. All of the research studies I am currently working on would benefit from another author, and I have the ability to help them reach their personal goals through that work.

4. How often should I assess my feelings about research?

    I do not think my motivators change that frequently, but reflecting once a month would be ideal. I should examine what gets me excited and put a plan in place to ensure those motivators are available for my work.

Continuing Education Units (CEUs)

A final benefit of publishing is the opportunity to obtain CEUs. Several years ago, the Behavior Analyst Certification Board changed continuing education requirements for BCBAs. The three categories of CEUs include learning, teaching, and scholarship. The scholarship activity allows behavior analysts to obtain CEUs for scholarly activities including publishing and completing reviews and serving as an action editor for behavior analytic journals. If you are starting out in the field, the publishing area will be the most obtainable. You can earn eight CEUs for one publication within your two-year continuing education cycle. This covers a significant portion of the thirty-two CEUs required. Additionally, as you progress in your career, you will likely find that reading, writing, and conducting your own research facilitates your continued learning in a unique way that attending events or other activities may not.

Essential Takeaways

To conclude, there are numerous benefits, both to you personally and to the field, of making a contribution to the literature as an applied researcher. For ease of use, appendix A provides all the questions listed above for each area of benefit in one worksheet. You can also download this worksheet at http://www.newharbinger.com/47827. These questions will allow you to look at your clinical practice and identify both the problems you are facing and the insight you can gain through research. Next, since the importance of ethics in research cannot be overstated, we'll spend two chapters on this topic.

CHAPTER 3

Ethics and Research

Before getting into the specifics about how to establish a research culture and resources at your organization, it is important to discuss the foundation of ethics that should serve as a base for the applied research you conduct. In 2020, the Behavior Analyst Certification Board (BACB) issued a new ethics code for behavior analysts, to be effective in early 2022. In this chapter, I'll delve into the newest professional and ethical compliance code for behavior analysts and how to comply with it. Then we will explore several scenarios involving ethical issues that researchers often face and recommendations for addressing these issues.

The Ethics Code and Research

The ethics code has one entire section (section 6) dedicated to behavior analysts and responsibility in research. The code discusses several areas of focus for researchers. Below, I list each subsection of this code and provide some interpretation as well as simple things you can do to adhere to the code fully while still conducting relevant applied research. The recommendations are not exhaustive but will get you started with specific actions you can engage in to support your initial research activities while building an ethical research culture. The code covers a variety of areas (some of which we've discussed in this book already), including having studies approved by a research review committee and how to ethically conduct research in the context of service delivery. Ethical issues will always arise, but knowledge of and compliance with the code will help you minimize them and, more importantly, establish communication with all parties when ethical issues happen.

6.01 Conforming with Laws and Regulations in Research. "Behavior analysts plan and conduct *research* in a manner consistent with all applicable laws and regulations, as well as requirements by organizations and institutions governing research activity."

　　How to comply: It is difficult to create an exhaustive list of all laws that might apply to you in your state. However, knowledge of some basic laws related to professionals who provide care to children is important. This is an area in which you will likely build resources and then add to them over the years as you become aware of other relevant laws and state regulations. Start a list of laws you are aware of that might impact your research agenda. Consult with the human resources leader in your organization and establish a foundation of information that you can add to over time. If your organization does not have this already, providing training on being a mandated reporter is relevant in all states and should be a part of any training that one receives to conduct research (or to provide any type of clinical care).

6.02 Research Review. "Behavior analysts conduct research, whether independent or in the context of service delivery, only after approval by a formal *research review committee*."

How to comply: Luckily, there are many resources to help you establish a formal research review committee or identify support from another organization's or institution's review committee. In chapter 4, I'll provide direction, templates, and several other resources to support you in adhering to this specific ethics code.

6.03 Research in Service Delivery. "Behavior analysts conducting research in the context of service delivery must arrange research activities such that client services and client welfare are prioritized. In these situations, behavior analysts must comply with all ethics requirements for both service delivery and research within the Code. When professional services are offered as an incentive for research participation, behavior analysts clarify the nature of services, and any potential risks, obligation, and limitations of all parties."

How to comply: In many ways, the topic of this book is centered on how to comply with this specific code. By conducting research that aligns with the clinical mission of an organization, and in the context of service delivery, clinical care and research questions can align well. Applied researchers should work to ensure the answers provided to research questions support clinical goals for each client. Having a research review committee in place, which I'll discuss in detail in chapter 4, can serve as a protective layer to ensure client welfare is prioritized.

6.04 Informed Consent in Research. "Behavior analysts are responsible for obtaining *informed consent* (and assent when relevant) from potential research participants under the conditions required by the research review committee. When behavior analysts become aware that data obtained from past or current clients, *stakeholders, supervisees and/or trainees* during typical service delivery might be disseminated to the scientific community, they obtain informed consent for use of the data before dissemination, specify that services will not be impacted by providing or withholding consent and make available the right to withdraw consent at any time without penalty."

How to comply: Create informed consent documents that are easy to read, and, when possible, embed basic language into existing consent forms (see chapter 4 for details). Take the time to explain the informed consent document, in person when possible. Treat the documentation as a conversation rather than a "read and sign" task; otherwise, most people will not read it fully and may be surprised to learn of something later in treatment that was outlined in the document. Answer all questions participants have and be sure to let the participant know that their willingness to participate does not influence the services they receive from your organization.

6.05 Confidentiality in Research. "Behavior analysts prioritize the confidentiality of their research participants except under conditions where it may not be possible. They make appropriate efforts to prevent accidental or inadvertent sharing of confidential information while conducting research and in any dissemination activity related to the research (e.g., disguising or removing confidential or identifying information).

How to comply: Use random numerical or alphanumerical codes for participants in a research study. Store data in a secure file and limit access to only people directly involved in the study. Avoid using names or other identifying information when writing or speaking about the research study. Provide training to any team members prior to their involvement in a research study to make them aware of processes involved in protecting confidentiality and of our ethical obligation to protect confidentiality. If a breach of confidentiality occurs, notify the participant(s) and change processes to prevent similar breaches in the future. Inform the participants and team members involved in the data breach of the occurrence.

6.06 Competence in Conducting Research. "Behavior analysts only conduct research independently after they have successfully conducted research under a supervisor in a defined relationship (e.g., thesis, dissertation, mentored research project). Behavior analysts and their assistants are permitted to perform only those research activities for which they are appropriately trained and prepared. Before engaging in research activities for which a behavior analyst has not received training, they seek the appropriate training and become demonstrably competent or they collaborate with other professionals who have the required competence. Behavior analysts are responsible for the ethical conduct of all personnel assigned to the research project."

How to comply: This section of the code clearly describes what you should do to ensure competence. If you've conducted research as part of your graduate program, you likely meet the basic requirements to have done so under some supervision. If you have never conducted research, you should seek mentorship (see chapter 8 for specific guidance on finding a research mentor). Even if you have conducted some research, you may not be equipped to conduct research independently and, early in your research endeavors, you may still seek support and mentorship. If you venture into an area that you do not have any background in, just as in clinical practice, you should seek appropriate training and consultation with professionals who have that knowledge. Finally, be sure to provide training to all individuals involved in your research study to be sure they understand the scope of their responsibilities, can act ethically, and manage research data appropriately.

6.07 Conflict of Interest in Research and Publication. "When conducting research, behavior analysts identify, disclose, and address *conflicts of interest* (e.g., personal, financial, organization related, service related). They also identify, disclose, and address conflicts of interest in their publication and editorial activities."

How to comply: The best tip here is to be aware of any special connection you may have to the research question, participants, or outcomes of the research study. If you identify such a connection, talk to peers, mentors, and the research review committee to determine if it represents a conflict of interest. If it indeed does, disclose that conflict in any form in which the research findings are made available (through presentations, publications). In some cases, the conflict of interest will bias your ability to act objectively. In these cases, you may need to remove yourself from the project or work to minimize the conflict so that you can remain objective.

6.08 Appropriate Credit. "Behavior analysts give appropriate credit (e.g., authorship, author-note acknowledgment) to research contributors in all dissemination activities. Authorship and other publication acknowledgments accurately reflect the relative scientific or professional contributions of the individuals involved, regardless of their professional status (e.g., professor, student)."

How to comply: At the beginning of a research study, have a conversation with all parties to discuss the order of authorship. This is important—research team members may enter the project thinking they have a higher authorship level than you intend them to, or thinking their role is less significant than it is. Some team members may expect authorship, but you or another coauthor may not think their contribution warrants it. Involve neutral third parties (mentors, research review committee) to help determine contribution if needed. Discuss authorship and your conclusions about it early in the research study development. Discuss these issues with everyone involved and document your decisions. You can always reassess; if someone decides they do not want to be a part of the study anymore or they want to play a more prominent role, you can work with the team to adjust the order of authorship.

6.09 Plagiarism. "Behavior analysts do not present portions or elements of another's work or data as their own. Behavior analysts only republish their previously published data or text when accompanied by proper disclosure."

How to comply: Always properly cite others' work. Provide training to those involved in writing your results to ensure they understand plagiarism and avoid engaging in it. If you ever question whether you need to cite something, do so and, if necessary, provide disclosures.

6.10 Documentation and Data Retention in Research. "Behavior analysts must be knowledgeable about and comply with all applicable standards (e.g., BACB rules, laws, research review committee requirements) for storing, transporting, retaining, and destroying physical and electronic documentation related to research. They retain identifying documentation and data for the longest required duration. Behavior analysts destroy physical documentation after making deidentified digital copies or summaries of data (e.g., reports and graphs) when permitted by relevant entities."

How to comply: There are several laws and regulations that require retaining information for varying amounts of time. Become familiar with any such laws in your state and with BACB ethical codes 2.03, 2.05, 3.11, and 4.05 addressing this issue. Create a process to retain records for the length of time that is longest according to these sources. It may also be helpful to add some extra time (e.g., six months to one year) to account for differing start and end times of research studies if it's possible to do so. If you exit an organization, be sure the organization knows the guidelines and rules on retaining the data for the specified time, even after your departure.

6.11 Accuracy and Use of Data. "Behavior analysts do not fabricate data or falsify results in their research, publications, and presentations. They plan and carry out their research and describe their procedures and findings to minimize the possibility that their research and results will be misleading or misinterpreted. If they discover errors in their published data, they take steps to correct them by following publisher policy. Data from research projects are presented to the public and scientific community in their entirety whenever possible. When that is not possible, behavior analysts take caution and explain the exclusion of data (whether single data points, or partial or whole data sets) from presentations or manuscripts submitted for publication by providing a rationale and description of what was excluded."

How to comply: Always be honest about your data and teach others to do the same. It may be tempting to rationalize removal of a data point or to change something like interobserver agreement (IOA) percentages to reflect your work in a positive light—but never, ever, ever do this. Teach others about the importance of honesty and the implications of inaccurate data reporting. If any inaccuracy is ever brought to your attention, address it immediately by following up with the journal (if the work is published), educating the team member (possibly taking corrective action with their employer and/or the BACB if the situation is severe and the act was intentional, despite the person's being aware of the code of conduct), and correcting the interpretation of the data.

Although the ethics code may seem overwhelming, you can adhere to it by establishing a strong research infrastructure with documentation, oversight, transparency, honesty, and support. The next chapter explains exactly how to do these things.

Research Ethics Scenarios and Recommendations

I want to present some ethical scenarios that you might encounter during your applied research activities and discuss solutions. Of course, you will not always have the exact part of the code memorized and you do not need to! Simply being willing to reference, seek consultation, and be truthful will enable you to act ethically. Professional ethics are never black and white, and research ethics are no different. Acting ethically also does not mean never having an ethical dilemma—in fact, it likely means the opposite! When you are aware of situations that may arise and knowledgeable of the code, you find more instances to respond to and educate others on. This is especially true for research conducted in applied settings. Read through the following ethical scenarios and take a moment to think through how you would respond. Then, read the recommendations for action to check your initial response.

Scenario 1

After beginning a research study on establishing vocal language in young learners with autism, you notice that two of your three participants have begun engaging in problem behavior that they had not previously engaged in. The procedures include a delay to reinforcement, and when you observe the session, you notice that during that delay, the participants both engage in aggression toward the data collector and implementer. Furthermore, when the research team follows the protocol, they seem to be reinforcing this problem behavior by providing access to preferred edible items. You did not anticipate this response, and nobody on the research review committee considered it might occur. One of the parents noticed it and asked how it could be corrected.

Recommended Action and Relevant Ethics Code(s): Code 6.03, Research in Service Delivery, and Code 6.04, Informed Consent in Research, are most relevant here. Stop research activity for all participants, including the one who has not yet engaged in problem behavior. Explain to the parents that the problem behavior was unexpected, and you want to discuss the situation with the research review committee (RRC) to get their advice on how to proceed. Email the RRC and ask to have a meeting to discuss the issue. At the meeting, present the situation to them and share data describing what you have observed. During that meeting, the RRC team members can provide advice about how to adapt the protocol (if possible) while maintaining the integrity of the experimental question. The committee can advise you about how to communicate to the parents, how to appropriately stop the research study if you need to do so, and how to mitigate additional risks. Understandably, some of the parents may express disappointment because the study was investigating ways to establish vocal speech. If it is determined that the study needs to stop, be prepared to discuss alternative options for clinical interventions to develop that skill.

Scenario 2

A member of your research team was responsible for uploading data to a data base after collecting it after each session. After one session, she accidentally uploaded the file to a different folder, one that all BCBAs in the company have access to. The file revealed some identifying information about the client. She did not realize the mistake until a few days later and saw that it had been downloaded a few times by BCBAs not involved in the research project. She brought it to your attention immediately after realizing the mistake.

Recommended Action and Relevant Ethics Code(s): Code 6.05 Confidentiality in Research, is most relevant here. Remove the file from the incorrect drive and place it in the secure folder. Follow up with the team member and provide extra training if needed. Follow up with the parent of the participant or the participant themself and inform them of the incident, as well as the action you took to correct it. Follow up with the team members not on the research team who accessed the file and ask them to keep the information confidential and to delete any copies of the file they made. Report the incident to the RRC and document its occurrence as well as the actions you took to resolve it.

Scenario 3

You submitted a study and received an "accept with revisions" decision from the associate editor (AE), meaning the study will be published if you make several revisions based on recommendations from the review panel and AE. As you are working through the revisions requested by the AE, you notice in the raw data that there are two data points that were never entered into the graph and thus never visually inspected. You enter the data and visually inspect it—it does not change the interpretation significantly but changes how you discuss the results and demonstrates slightly less experimental control.

Recommended Action and Relevant Ethics Code(s): Code 6.11, Accuracy and Use of Data, comes to play in this scenario. Follow up with the AE and describe the oversight. Present the new data and a plan to address it in the revised manuscript, including how your interpretation of the data will change. Allow the AE to guide you in next steps, which might include submitting your paper to a new review panel or upholding the decision to accept the paper pending revisions. The AE will likely have some recommendations for how to describe the data based on the new information and regarding your results.

It is important to note here that you might be tempted to ignore this oversight altogether, convincing yourself that the data didn't change much, and nobody will ever know about that missing data—do not do this!! The ethical decision here is to acknowledge the mistake and communicate with the AE. You should never present false data to the scientific community—it will influence consumers experiencing the procedure, researchers wishing to replicate your results, and research that builds upon yours. You do not want (nor are you ethically allowed) to have those activities be based on inaccurate data.

Scenario 4

You arrive at a participant's home to observe a therapist conducting a research session and to collect IOA data. When discussing the project with the participant's mother, you notice that she is acting a bit differently about the project. Before she was very excited and asked a lot of questions; now she seems negative and reserved. You directly ask her what is going on. She states that she does not like the procedures and wants to withdraw from the study. She said she mentioned her desire to withdraw to the therapist, who told her that she was not able to withdraw without it impacting her regular clinical services.

Recommended Action and Relevant Ethics Code(s): Code 6.04, Informed Consent in Research, gives guidance here. Tell the parent right away that she can withdraw from the study and her decision will not impact her services in any way. Immediately after the session, follow up with the therapist and let her know that her behavior was inappropriate and inaccurate. Have her retake a training on research ethics. Follow up after she has completed the training and assess her understanding. Do not allow her to work on any other research projects until she completes the training and demonstrates understanding of the behavior and how to respond differently in the future.

Scenario 5

You had asked a junior member of your research team to write the discussion section of a research study, and it reads very well. You notice a few sentences in the discussion section that sound very familiar. After further research, you realize that there are three sentences that are nearly identical to three sentences in another research study you published a few years ago on a similar topic, but no reference is provided. When you follow up with the research team member, he says that since you wrote the study and were an author on the current one, he did not think he needed to cite it. He did not realize there would be any problem with this situation.

Recommended Action and Relevant Ethics Code(s): Code 6.09, Plagiarism, is relevant in this scenario. Inform the team member that even though it is something you wrote, it is inappropriate to copy it word for word. Also inform him that although you are an author on both papers, citation is still necessary. Assess his understanding and provide oversight of his writing in future work. This is how some plagiarism can occur—it is very rarely intentional reproduction of someone else's work without citation (though this sometimes occurs). Plagiarism usually happens due to lack of knowledge—either that something needed to be cited properly or a mistaken belief that the idea was not original enough to warrant it as an independent thought.

Scenario 6

A company reaches out to you about a new app they want to test for teaching children with autism. You think the app is interesting and could make a good research study. You work with the company to establish a plan to propose the study to your RRC. The company offers to give you the app for free for all of the families served by your company, but only if the study shows positive results.

Recommended Action and Relevant Ethics Code(s): Code 6.07, Conflict of Interest in Research and Publication, is relevant in deciding how to respond. Explain to the company that you are conducting research and cannot control the results of the study. Let them know that you cannot accept the app for free under certain conditions about how the data turn out. They can provide the app for free for use for the study, but they cannot make it available in exchange for conducting the study and certainly not for getting certain results. Be sure the company is disconnected from the daily management of the research data, except as it relates to the technicalities of use of the app. In any presentations and publications, you should acknowledge the company's provision of the app to participants and disclose their involvement in the study.

Scenario 7

You have a member on your research team who also provides some direct care to several families. He has worked with you to develop a research study, and you are getting ready to present the study to the RRC for approval. Shortly before the RRC meeting, you find out that he began implementing the study procedures with several of his clients. When you approach him about this, he expresses his sincere apologies and states that he did not know he could not get started until the RRC approved it.

Recommended Action and Relevant Ethics Code(s): Code 6.02, Research Review, informs the decision here. Although this individual is not certified, you have accountability for his actions because you are certified, and he is working on a research study for you. Inform him that all studies must go through the RRC before they can be conducted. Explain that this is important because changes might occur based on the RRC's review, and the protocol and informed consent documents could be different. Explain to the parent that we cannot proceed with the research study until it is approved, apologizing for the inconvenience and any misunderstanding. When you meet with the RRC, explain the situation to them and seek guidance. The RRC will direct you on how to appropriately debrief with the family. They will also tell you how you should adapt the study's procedures based the client's premature start. For example, the client may need to be excluded from the study, or, after RRC review, the procedures may need to change and therefore the data collected so far would not be able to be used.

Scenario 8

You conducted a study on sleep training for individuals with autism and published it in a more mainstream, non-behavior analytic journal. You hear that your work is going to be discussed on a podcast about child-rearing. When you listen to the podcast, you find out that the host incorrectly described the results of your study, suggesting something that the data did not support. The podcast has already been broadcast and people are beginning to contact you with questions about how to sleep train their child.

Recommended Action and Relevant Ethics Code(s): Code 6.11, Accuracy and Use of Data, is relevant. In this situation, you should contact the host of the podcast and inform them of the inaccuracy. Ask that you be given an opportunity to go on their show or issue a statement that they read correcting the interpretation of your data. If they are unwilling, you could prepare a response and post it on your own personal web page, blog, or social media sites. You could also respond to any inquiries with that statement, correcting the misinterpretation.

Scenario 9

A student who was completing a practicum placement at your organization under your supervision helped organize data for a study that later got published. You did not have a conversation with her about acknowledgement or authorship because you did not think the contribution was worthy of authorship. She followed up with you after the study was published and asked why she was not provided authorship given her contribution.

Recommended Action and Relevant Ethics Code(s): Code 6.08, Appropriate Credit, pertains to this issue. Respond to her and apologize for the misunderstanding. Explain your perspective and interpretation of the standards in the field for what constitutes a contribution warranting authorship. If she understands your perspective, you could offer her an acknowledgement. Follow up with the journal to see if you can have this added after the fact into the acknowledgment section of your publication. Although it may be too late to correct the printed version, you could modify the online article with this verbiage. In the future, remember to have conversations with every person involved in research studies to avoid this type of misunderstanding. Make it very clear to everyone who helps on a study what their role is and their opportunities for authorship. Address any disagreements or changes throughout the project as they arise.

Scenario 10

You accept a new position in an organization. The position is a higher level one, with partial clinical and partial research responsibilities. You quickly identify that the staff have not conducted research before and need a significant amount of training both on the ethical research practices and on how to conduct research in an applied setting. Upon initial discussion with the organization's leadership, they show some hesitancy with allotting your proposed amount of training time to research.

Recommended Action and Relevant Ethics Code(s): Code 6.06 Competence in Conducting Research, will be applicable to this scenario. It would be appropriate for you to review your proposal to identify any ways you could make your training more efficient (e.g., training a smaller number of focused research group members, combining topics, incorporating ethical research practices into existing policies and processes). However, you should not compromise on the need to train the staff on research practices. Use the ethics code to discuss the need with the company's leadership and collaborate on a plan that will be easily integrated into the business while still upholding your responsibility to provide training to individuals in the company who will participate in research.

To conclude, you should not be afraid of ethical issues arising in your research—they are unavoidable and, in many ways, out of your control. In fact, if a behavior analyst tells you they've never encountered any ethical dilemmas, they are likely not aware of ethics that surround their practice or their research. The important part of research and the thing you can control is how you respond when ethical issues arise. The keys to responding appropriately and mitigating risk are to consult with peers, communicate, be honest, and adjust future behavior based on what you learn from the dilemma.

Can you anticipate any ethical dilemmas you might face while pursuing you research plan? List them here:

_____

_____

_____

_____

_____

What are some ways you can ensure that when ethical issues arise, they are addressed quickly and appropriately? Examples include training, communication, and maintaining a research review committee.

_____

_____

_____

_____

Essential Takeaways

It can feel a bit intimidating to incorporate research into your applied work in a way that is ethical and consistent with our professional code of conduct. Try not to get overwhelmed by this. You already practice ethically each day—the task here is simply to extend your knowledge of and compliance with the ethics code to a new activity and way of thinking about your clinical work. Use the resources in this chapter to get started and always reach out to colleagues for support as you go along.

CHAPTER 4

Ethical Oversight

When writing this book, I initially planned to cover all aspects of ethics in one chapter. However, the topic of ethical oversight is so important that it warrants its own chapter. Having reviewed the part of the BACB ethics code pertaining to research, you'll be better equipped to consider the issues of oversight I'll present in this chapter. Conducting research in applied settings presents some logistical challenges that may discourage practitioners from pursuing their research interests. One of the barriers to conducting research that practitioners report is lack of access to an institutional review board or research review committee (Valentino & Juanico, 2020), the two primary types of governing boards. However, this barrier can be overcome with some creativity and support from others. In this chapter, we'll look at what the different governing bodies are, why they exist, and ways to overcome the governing body barrier, including the steps to establish your own.

Governing Bodies

An institutional review board (IRB) is a third-party group of individuals whose purpose is to ensure the rights and protections of human participants in research studies. Their main goal is to minimize risk to participants, ensure their safety, and promote ethical research practices. You may be familiar with an IRB if you completed a master's thesis that involved human participants. An IRB typically oversees research conducted by individuals at an institution, such as a university or hospital. The IRB is a wonderful resource for students and individuals working in academia and for practitioners collaborating with someone affiliated with those institutions. However, once a student graduates or a professional is no longer affiliated with a university, this resource is typically not available. Thus, individuals wishing to ethically conduct research outside of a university setting may encounter this barrier and not see a way to conduct research without an IRB.

A research review committee (RRC) is an independent review board established by independent agencies or groups of people to ensure ethical research practices with vulnerable populations (LeBlanc et al., 2018). As outlined in our discipline's code of ethics, review by a research committee is required by the BACB for anyone conducting research (BACB, 2020). An RRC can serve the same purpose for private agencies as an IRB does for universities or other large institutions such as hospitals. The RRC typically consists of a variety of individuals, some of whom are nonscientific, some nonaffiliated, and some scientists and experts. LeBlanc et al. (2018) outline the history and legal requirements surrounding an

RRC and specific details about how to establish one. I recommend that you read the LeBlanc paper for these details and a "how to" guide. You may be able to access an RRC through another organization, or you can establish one internally on your own.

Most for-profit companies are unlikely to have an established RRC for several reasons. First, they may not be aware that practitioners are capable of and interested in conducting research. Thus, establishing an RRC may not be a priority. Second, many organizations may not know how to establish an RRC. Finally, having an RRC requires a time commitment from the committee as well as from those participating in research, and organizations may be reluctant to commit that time to the cause.

Although it is uncommon for an organization to have an RRC, it is incredibly important and necessary to have one when conducting applied research any time human participants are involved. If you or your colleagues are conducting research during service delivery (as is most often the case in applied settings), you must be very cautious to avoid engaging in any activities that do not benefit the consumer. And if you don't know whether there will be a benefit or not, you must take appropriate precautions and obtain consent. It is very easy to fail to recognize risks that may be present in a study you are involved in. You might be committed to the research question and to conducting research, thus proceeding without realizing that the procedures are experimental or even pose a risk. The RRC can provide an independent and objective review so you can be sure you proceed ethically. In my own practice and research, all studies conducted at our organization go through the RRC if human participants are involved. Even for studies that seemingly involve minimal risk (e.g., experimental evaluation of a new app for data coding), we seek some level of review from the RRC. It is always refreshing to hear from the committee, and, given the variety of expertise present on the panel, they often bring up considerations that the research team has not taken into account. The RRC provides an extra level of protection and allows the researchers to proceed with confidence.

Now that you know a bit more about the governing bodies, their purpose, and the importance of committee review, you may still be concerned that you will not be able to establish an RRC or gain access to one to proceed with your research interests. Below, I offer several ways you can conduct research and overcome this barrier, and even establish an RRC on your own.

Establish an RRC at Your Organization

The first and most obvious way to ensure that you have access to a governing body is to establish an RRC at your organization. Here is a step-by step process for establishing an RRC. I will list each step and then discuss the steps in detail, offering templates and discussion starters for you to use to accomplish each step. I'll provide examples of many of these resources to get you started.

1. Select and train members of your research review committee.

2. Speak to the leaders in your organization about carving out time.

3. Develop a research policy.

4. Develop a research study application.

5. Ask your leadership team to include consent language in your informed consent for services document.

6. Create a template for study-specific research consent.

7. Create an annual renewal and review process.

8. Set a structure for your RRC meeting.

9. Train your researchers.

Step 1: Select and train members of your research review committee. You may be surprised at how easy it is to construct an RRC and how willing individuals are to sit on the committee. In the eight plus years that the RRC has been in existence at my organization, I have never had anyone (internal or external to the organization) decline the request to sit on the committee. Although it is an unpaid position, the time commitment is usually minimal, and professionals are typically eager to help while being genuinely interested in the research happening in the field. The service can be beneficial to them too—behavior analyst committee members may engage with clinicians who will become future master's level or PhD students and are likely to get research ideas from the applied issues discussed. Non-behavior analyst members can learn more about the field, make professional connections, and use the committee as an example of community service. If you need assistance designing the committee, reach out to a senior member of your organization and explain what you'd like to do. They may have connections and even be willing to serve on the committee and/or help you set it up.

LeBlanc et al. (2018) provide an excellent guide on the requirements for committee members and the profile of individuals to choose; they also provide recommendations on training the committee members. You will need to identify a chair of the committee (perhaps you), who will take responsibility for receiving proposals, maintaining documentation, and organizing meetings. Having one or two individuals with a background in human resources (HR) can be useful, particularly if some of your research projects involve team members as participants. These committee members have a vast amount of knowledge about labor laws and team member rights that many behavior analysts likely do not have. Internal HR team members will also be familiar with company policies and procedures—they can consider if research proposals will be commensurate with company policies and if consent should be written into onboarding documentation to allow research to be conducted with team members upon employment. You can also consider having a committee member in training—a junior team member who is interested in learning about research. This individual can support the chair in taking notes and organizing information while learning. They may eventually become a full committee member and possibly the chair of the committee. The committee should be composed of approximately five to seven members. Here is an example of a committee makeup:

- **External Member:** *University professor, behavior analyst, chair of university IRB*

- **External Member:** *Past employee, human resources director*

- **External Member:** *Executive advisor, behavior analyst, past RRC director*

- **Internal Member:** *Executive team member, business background*

- **Internal Member:** *Current employee, human resources manager*

- **Internal Member:** *Chair, behavior analyst, executive team member*

- **Internal Team Members in Training**—*Postdoctoral fellow, behavior analyst*

Spend a few moments listing the people you might ask to fill each role. If you do not have specific names, think about the ideal background, training, and personality characteristics of someone you would want in that role.

- **External Member:** _____

- **External Member:** _____

- **External Member:** _____

- **Internal Member:** _____

- **Internal Member:** _____

- **Internal Member:** _____

- **Internal Team Members in Training:** _____

Step 2: Speak to the leaders in your organization about carving out time. Later in this chapter, I will describe some of the policies and processes involved in organizing and maintaining an RRC. These will take some work to develop and maintain—work that is above and beyond your day job. Consider talking with your direct supervisor and/or the executive members at your organization. Explain what you would like to do and the potential benefits to the organization (e.g., reduced turnover, increased team member engagement, positive reputation in the field), and see if they would be willing to carve out some time for you to lead these efforts. This support could be in the form of extra pay for your efforts, a reduced caseload, or simply dedicated time during your work each month to support research. Here are some talking points you can use to discuss your interest with your organization. Remember, not all companies will see the value in their clinicians conducting research, and they may even view it as a distraction. Thus, you must highlight the value to the organization and ways in which you'll not only minimize disruption to client services, but positively augment them.

Talking points for discussing beginning research at your organization:

- Research can help the organization stand out. This can be valuable to prospective team members and to families seeking services.

- The ability to conduct research can be very appealing to team members—especially BCBAs. Having a research infrastructure may help the organization attract and retain great employees.

- Conducting research will help team members become better practitioners.

- Single-subject research can be conducted during clinical work. Thus, the clinician's attention will not be diverted from client service delivery.

- Having a presence at conferences and in journals can support the positive image of the organization over time.

- Materials (e.g., consent forms, research requests, research protocol templates) can be created for use multiple times to minimize workload.

- Having even a small research presence is of little to no cost to the organization.

Take a few moments to write some of your own talking points, unique to your company and to your organization. List them here:

_____

_____

_____

_____

_____

Step 3: Develop a research policy. It is important for your organization to develop a research policy so that employees in the company know what types of research they can conduct, whom to contact if they want to conduct research, and how to engage in the process. Your research policy should describe the following:

- The purpose of the policy

- Whom the policy applies to (i.e., the scope)

- Step-by-step guide on how to comply with the policy

- Whom to contact with questions

- Links to other related policies

- Any other areas that are noteworthy

Your organization's policy will need to be individualized based on the people involved, oversight, types of consumers, and overall support for research. Most policies should include a purpose and specific steps for employees to follow. To view a sample research policy, see appendix B, which contains the research policy developed for Trumpet Behavioral Health (TBH), the organization I work for.

Below is a template you can use to assist in creating your organization's research policy. You can download this template at http://www.newharbinger.com/47827 to use as the foundation of your document.

Research Policy Template

Purpose

The purpose of this policy is to _____. This policy links to our core values in the following ways:

Scope

This policy applies to _____ [include the people and the research it pertains to].

Policy

To conduct research at _____ [name of organization], follow these steps:

Other things to note

Once the research policy is developed, the remaining steps will assist you in establishing compliance with this policy.

Step 4: Develop a research study application. Create an application for individuals wishing to conduct research. This is an important document for the RRC to help them understand the project. It serves as formal documentation regarding the procedural details that the researcher(s) have committed to. Additionally, this document can help the researcher(s) consider all the variables involved in conducting their study, including risks and benefits. The RRC study application should be two to four pages in length and provide an overview of each section. Appendix C contains a sample of an initial RRC study application. You can also download this sample application at http://www.newharbinger.com/47827. Tailor the document to your organization's needs, but focus on procedures, population, risks, benefits, and any known conflicts of interest. The application should be written in a way that both behavior analysts and non-behavior analysts can understand. Avoid excessive use of technical jargon and include important procedural details about what participants will experience before, during, and after your study. Finally, if you are collaborating with another institution, both organizations will want to see each other's approval letters and related documents. This can be a bit tricky if each organization wants the other to review the proposal first. When this conflict occurs, you can typically speak with each organization to determine how best to sequence the proposals with each institution. Typically, one organization will agree to review the proposal first and will request that the final documents from the other organization be submitted before participant recruitment begins.

In general, the topics contained in a research study application are as follows:

- Basic Information:

  · Primary researcher's name and position

  · Names and positions of other researchers involved in the study

  · Type of research (internal research request, external research request, use of archival data, formal research protocol)

  · Title of study

  · Intended location(s) of study

  · Date of submission

  · Anticipated start date of planned project

- Project-Specific Information

  · Rationale for and introduction to the study

  · Method

  · Results

  · Risks and benefits

  · References

  · Attachments

Step 5: Ask your leadership team to include consent language in your informed consent for services document. There may be several research projects that are so consistent with clinical work that the idea to present and/or publish does not come until after the data have been collected. An example of this situation involved research conducted by Veazey, Valentino, Low, McElroy, and LeBlanc in 2016. These authors taught menstrual-care skills to two clients with disabilities. The protocol was based on the literature, but the most recent article on this topic was published over thirty years ago. Thus, Veazey and her colleagues updated the protocol to be consistent with modern menstrual-care supplies and to be implemented with younger participants in the home environment. When the data set was complete, the results were promising, and it was evident that the data would make a great contribution to the field. So, after confirming with the RRC that appropriate consent for publication was obtained in the initial client paperwork, they sought and obtained research publication in the journal *Behavior Analysis in Practice.* You may be in other situations (e.g., combining outcomes or comparing prompting strategies) that are similar to the experience of Veazey and her colleagues, and you decide you want to seek publication after your analysis or clinical work is complete. In these cases, it would be very difficult—and may not be necessary—to obtain retrospective consent from every consumer. However, some form of consent for publication and presentation is still necessary. Your organization can include standard language in its main informed consent document that would allow all consumers to consent to presentation and publication of their de-identified data when it is a standard part of clinical service delivery. Here is an example of that type of language:

Research

Research is unique in the field of applied behavior analysis in that it sometimes can be accomplished during clinical services. Team members at our organization sometimes evaluate the effects of different aspects of our practice. We might review past data and summarize findings for services that have already occurred. Data are confidential. We may publish or present these data.. If we wish to conduct research that involves a specific protocol that is different from your standard clinical service delivery, we will obtain unique informed consent to do so from you before proceeding. All data collected are kept confidential, and anonymity is protected during presentations and publications.

Step 6: Create a template for study-specific research consent. When specific informed consent is needed, the researchers should develop a separate form. The consent form should be written in simple language at approximately a fifth-grade reading level and should be translated into the primary language of the participant. The consent form should inform the participant of exactly what they will experience and the risks and benefits of participating and should include a clear statement that they can withdraw at any time and services will not be impacted. Here are some sections that are common to include in a study-specific consent form, with instructions about how to complete each section.

Study Research Consent

Introduction

Provide a general overview of the purpose of this document (to review consent) and about the way in which this family was chosen to participate.

What is this study about?

Describe the study in language that does not involve technical jargon and explain why it is important.

What does it mean to participate in the study?

Describe what the parent/guardian is committing to in terms of time, activity, and duration of study. What, if anything, will be different about the child's sessions as a result of participation?

Are there any risks?

If so, describe them here.

Are there any benefits?

If so, describe them here.

Will anyone know we are participating?

Describe anonymity and how it will be protected. Discuss coding and protection of data storage, and how personal information will be protected if the study is presented or published.

What if I change my mind?

Explain the process for withdrawing from the study and that the participant has the right to do so any time without impact on clinical services.

Who can I contact with questions or concerns?

List the primary researcher's contact information, and also list someone not involved in the study. Parents/guardians may feel more comfortable contacting someone with concerns if they are not one of the researchers on the study.

Step 7: Create an annual renewal and review process. Another useful resource is a process and application for the renewal of projects after they have been running for a certain period (typically one year). This document serves to prompt the researchers to let the RRC know of any changes to the protocol and any unanticipated risks or adverse events that occurred. The document also encourages researchers to formally notify the RRC if (and why) the project is complete or stops for another reason before completion. Below is an example of a process and application for annual review and renewal that has been used at Trumpet Behavioral Health.**

**   This sample document is being shared with the approval of Trumpet Behavioral Health and remains the property of TBH. Any reuse or publication of this document without the written consent of TBH is strictly prohibited.

[Company Name]

Process for Annual Research Review & Renewal

1. Upon acceptance of a project through the Research Review Committee (RRC), the chair will designate a renewal review date and inform the principal investigator (PI) of that date.

2. The chair of the RRC will review all projects (using and completing the form below in collaboration with the PI of the study) on an annual basis.

3. The chair will request information from the PI as needed to accurately complete the process.

4. If documentation is missing or there are errors, the chair will work with the PI to correct them. Examples of missing documentation or errors may include informed consent for a participant(s), outdated version of protocol, data files include participant identifying information, etc.

   If the PI remedies the error, no further action will be required

   If the PI fails to remedy the error, the chair will call a meeting with the RRC and consult with the committee about further action

5. If the chair identifies an error that poses a risk to the participants, she will call a meeting with the RRC and consult with the committee to help the PI remedy the situation.

Trumpet Behavioral Health Research Renewal Application

To be completed by Primary Researcher	
Principal investigator(s) full name(s):	
Title of Study:	
Please list all the people who have been actively involved in conducting this study and their role in the study (e.g., collection IOA data, scoring videos for PI) [if necessary, add additional rows]	
Name: Role:	Name: Role:
Total number of participants completed:	Select Number
Total number of participants in progress:	Select Number
Total number of participants who withdrew from study:	Select Number
Reason for withdrawal:	
Have there been any modifications to the protocol since it was initially approved by the Research Review Committee?	Select Yes or No
If yes, please describe:	
Have any additional problems or potential risks developed since your project was approved?	Select Yes or No
If yes, please describe:	
How much more time do you anticipate you will spend actively collecting data on this project (e.g., 6 months, 1 year)?	Select an item

The below information will be assessed by the chair of the RRC.

Please use it as a guide to ensure all the documentation for the project is present prior to the chair's review.

Updated protocol	☐
Updated data sheets	☐
Updated graph template	☐
Participant signed informed consent documents (completed, withdrew, and active participants)	☐
All participant data (completed, withdrew, and active participants)	☐
Data stored per consumer protections (i.e., participant number, not name or other identifying information)	☐
Interobserver Agreement Tracking System—included and up to date	☐
Procedural integrity tracking system—included and up to date	☐

Step 8: Set a structure for your RRC meeting. Developing a standardized communication to RRC members when a proposal needs to be reviewed can help the committee quickly respond and reduce the amount of effort on your part for each communication. You'll also need to develop a way to coordinate scheduling of the RRC meeting—preferably one that can be used across time zones and with individuals both inside and outside of your organization. The members of the committee are likely very busy and volunteering their time. Thus, you'll want to send the materials at least one week, and ideally two weeks, ahead of the scheduled meeting. This will give them ample time to review the materials so they are prepared to discuss the protocol(s). Finally, consider batching proposals together so that committee members do not have to meet frequently to review one protocol at a time. Typically, committees will meet twice per year (minimum) to quarterly (maximum).

Here is a sample email to committee members.

Hi Committee Members (include each one's name),

I hope this email finds you well! We have an internal project that is ready for review. The principal investigators are _____ and _____. I am attaching the materials for your review and would love to set up a time for them to present it to you, discuss the project, and seek approval.

Here is a link to a poll to gather everyone's availability. It should convert to your time zone, but just in case, the first time is Tuesday 10/1/19 at 9 a.m. Pacific Time. Please complete it at your earliest convenience. Please scroll all the way to the right and expand the view—there are lots of options!

(Insert link to scheduling here)

Thank you so much for continuing to support our organization!

If you have any questions, please let me know.

Best,

Amber

Once you've established a meeting time, it is important to create a structure for the meeting. This structure will ensure that the time is used effectively and that you are as efficient as possible. Depending on how many protocols are being reviewed, the meeting could be scheduled for thirty to ninety minutes. It is common for the principal investigator of each project to present their proposal and then leave the meeting so the committee can discuss it. Thus, you may have different people calling in at different times to present the proposals if you have more than one to review. It is also common to review the status of existing protocols at least once to twice per year so the committee is aware of each one, where it stands, and any adverse events that may have occurred since the initial approval. Here is a sample agenda for an RRC meeting that has two projects to be reviewed.

Research Review Committee (RRC) Meeting

October 1, 2019; 9 a.m.–10:20 a.m. Pacific Time

Time	Leader	Task
9:00 a.m.–9:15 a.m.	Amber Valentino	Introductions & Welcome
9:15 a.m.–9:30 a.m.	Jerry Seinfeld	Research Proposal "An examination of American sitcoms from the 1990s"
9:30 a.m.–9:45 a.m.	Harry Potter	Research Proposal "Comparison of two different strategies for becoming a wizard"
9:45 a.m.–10:00 a.m.	Amber Valentino	Discussion of both projects with Q&A
10:00 a.m.–10:05 a.m.	Amber Valentino	Voting of approval/denial/approval pending revisions for each project
10:05 a.m.–10:15 a.m.	Amber Valentino	Discussion of status of existing projects
10:15 a.m.–10:20 a.m.	Amber Valentino	Closing, future meetings, thank you

Once the committee has met and decided about each protocol, you'll need to document that decision and communicate it to the researchers. Typically, the committee can decide to approve the project as is, approve it with modifications (most common decision), or deny it. A pure denial is uncommon because the chair should work with the researchers prior to the meeting to get the protocol ready for review. If a project is too dangerous, the question has already been answered. If the procedures are flawed, the researchers can fix the protocol before it goes up for formal review to the committee or change the idea to be more conducive to the setting and/or minimize risks. Below are two sample response letters.

Sample Letter 1 (Approval as is)

4/15/16

To (Researcher),

The Research Review Committee of XYZ organization met on April 15, 2016, and reviewed the application for the project entitled **(Place title here)** *with* **(Researchers),** *listed as the primary investigators. After a review, this project was approved by the RRC and has full cooperation in recruiting participants, obtaining informed consent, and conducting the research at our agency in conjunction with XXX University.*

I am aware of the study's objectives and I believe that this research will facilitate evaluation of **(provide summary of study's aims)** *while serving the purpose of a research project.*

For the duration of the study, I will maintain contact with you as the primary researcher. Please direct all questions to me at **(email)** *or* **(phone).**

Sincerely,

Name

Title

Chair, Research Review Committee

Sample letter 2 (Approval with modifications)

10/16/19

Dear (Researchers),

The Research Review Committee (RRC) of XYZ organization met on October 16, 2019, and reviewed the application for your project entitled (Title). *After a review, the committee has conditionally approved your project, contingent upon the following additions:*

Create a consent form for team members that describes that (1) they have the right to withdraw from the study at any time and their employment will not be impacted by this decision in any way, (2) clinician data collected may be used for presentation and publication purposes (this is particularly relevant if you decide to collect social validity and/or demographic data from the team members), and (3) the researchers will keep client information confidential.

Solidify a plan for how to proceed if the clinician drops out of the study (e.g., the family will work with a different clinician on the case, a different researcher will step in). You can simply write this in your RRC application document.

These changes do not require full committee review—make them and send them directly to me once complete to proceed with collecting data.

Thank you for submitting your study to our RRC. For the duration of the study, I will maintain contact with you as the primary researcher. Please direct all questions to me at (insert contact information here).

Sincerely,

Name

Title

Chair, Research Review Committee

Step 9: Train your researchers. Finally, individuals participating in research should receive training on research ethics. The important components of training enable the researchers to be aware of any biases, to act with integrity, and to seek assistance navigating any conflicts that arise. I recommend developing a simple PowerPoint presentation with the main training points (listed below). For efficiency, organizations might consider recording the training so anyone can watch at any time. If the organization has access to a learning management system, you could develop an e-learning module; otherwise, using simple technology such as recording the training meeting would suffice.

Here is an outline of topics that could be included in a training:

- Company-specific resources and requirements including:

  · Research policy

  · Research Review Committee—make up and support

  · Study application

  · Consent

  · Annual review and renewal process

  · Structure for RRC meetings

- Definition of research

- The value of clinical research

- The company's philosophy on research

- Structural differences between good clinical work and research

- Definition of ethics

- History of research misconduct

- History of ethics regulations

- Requirements for human research

- Informed consent

All researchers obtaining informed consent should receive training on how to do so ethically. This can be accomplished using competency-based training materials and by giving team members the opportunity to practice obtaining consent through role-play. Here is a checklist of areas to cover when training team members to obtain informed consent.

Training Checklist: Informed Consent

- Cover the following points in conversation form and allow questions throughout the discussion.

- Explain the purpose of the discussion.

- Explain the purpose of the informed consent document.

- Explain what the study is about (research question).

- Review why the study is important.

- Describe each step of participation.

- Identify and explain any risks associated with participation, if applicable.

- Explain benefits of participation for the child/family and any other parties.

- Review assurance of confidentiality.

- Review where data may be presented.

- Explain that participation is 100% voluntary.

- Explain that clinical services are not impacted if the client declines to participate.

- Cover the right to withdraw from the study and that data collected can also be removed.

- Review how long data will be stored.

- Review whom to contact with questions.

- Ask if there are any questions; allow sufficient time and answer all questions before having the parent/guardian sign the informed consent document.

- Have the parent/guardian sign and date the form; you sign and date the form.

In the event that you decide to take a different path and not establish your own RRC, you can still conduct research ethically. Here are some ways in which you can accomplish conducting research without an internal RRC.

Utilize a University IRB

If establishing an RRC at your organization seems overwhelming or you've run into obstacles that prevent you from proceeding, consider utilizing a university IRB. One way to do this would be to partner with an academician or student affiliated with the university who may be interested in conducting the research with you. You can also consider asking the IRB if they would review the study even though you are not affiliated with their university. There may be a cost, but universities are likely willing to offer the service. There is no formal process for arranging for this. Simply determine the point of contact for the university's IRB and send them an email. If you happen to have a professional connection to someone at the university, you could ask them to introduce you to someone on the IRB or who can speak with you about collaboration. Here is a sample email you could send to someone at a university regarding support from their IRB.

Dear

_____,

My name is Amber Valentino and I am a behavior analyst with ABC Behavioral Health. I am a clinician and I support a caseload of 15 patients with autism. My organization is interested in conducting applied research. We currently do not have the ability to establish our own research review committee, so I am reaching out to you to ask about the possibility of utilizing your university IRB. If there is a fee associated with this, please let us know. We also want to be helpful to your university in any way we can—potentially setting up practicum sites and sharing our research resources with you. Thank you for your kind consideration of this request. If you need more information or want to talk further, please let me know.

Sincerely,

Amber

Other Types of Research

Finally, if an RRC or IRB is unavailable, you can consider other projects that do not involve human participants. There are many examples of these in the literature, and they have made great contributions over the years. Examples include literature reviews, which synthesize research on a topic (see Aguirre et al., 2016); treatment models, which demonstrate the way a group of practitioners or researchers approach a clinical issue, such as treatment of escape-maintained problem behavior (Geiger et al., 2010); or recommended practice guidelines, such as on how to approach supervision (Sellers, Valentino, & LeBlanc, 2016). When considering these types of projects, it is advisable to speak with leaders at your organization to ensure you do not share any materials or resources that are proprietary to the organization.

Essential Takeaways

Ethical oversight is critical in conducting research and must involve a governing body—an IRC or IRB—when human participants are involved. There are several activities and projects to tackle to organize research support in your organization, all of which are achievable. Tackle one thing at a time, prioritizing the precise tools you need to get started and moving through your list as needs arise. For example, of the tools we've discussed in this chapter, you will not need an established process and document for annual renewals right away, but you'll likely need to incorporate some research language into your informed consent document. Tackle the informed consent document first so this is not a barrier to beginning a research project in your organization. Tackling one thing at a time is a perfect segue to the next chapter, which is all about time management.

CHAPTER 5

Time Management and Staying Productive

In this chapter, I am going to discuss several time-management strategies to help you to persist with your research and stay organized. These strategies include creating a task analysis, planning and scheduling, taking data on your own research and writing behavior, and making data-based decisions. Before I discuss these and other behavioral recommendations, though, I'll help you differentiate between a skill deficit and a motivation deficit in relation to your research behavior and, very importantly, discuss time management and productivity in relation to your self-care and work-life balance. This chapter will set the framework for managing your time and staying productive as a researcher.

Skill Deficit vs. Motivation Deficit

When individuals struggle with time management and staying productive on a goal they've set for themselves, I find that it's not always the "how to" that's missing. That is, it's not a skill deficit. Many people know how to create to-do lists, allot time, and even accomplish some tasks related to their goal. In these cases, the issue is often motivation rather than lacking a specific skill set. Before proceeding to implement the practical strategies I recommend later in this book, first assess your motivation. You'll find that differentiating between a skill deficit and a motivation issue in yourself is not all that different from differentiating between these two issues in the clients with whom you work. Generally, if you can execute the skill with different tasks and at different times in any capacity, it's a motivation issue. If you never demonstrate the skill, even under optimal conditions of motivation, it is a skill deficit.

There are several questions you can ask yourself to help identify the underlying issue if you've been struggling to become (or remain) productive. As you read through these questions, you may venture into some self-discovery about your motivations to conduct applied research, and those motivators may be inconsistent with what you initially thought might motivate you. Over the years of mentoring others in applied research, I have met some individuals who, although they express interest in research, realize, when they really dig in, that they are not very motivated at all, or if they are motivated in some way, their motivators are distant and external (e.g., they think they should, their grad school professor encouraged them to publish in their career). These types of motivators are not amenable to a sustainable research career. Interestingly, some of these individuals picked research back up later in their careers when they were truly motivated to do so. Usually something changed in their life—they met a big personal or professional milestone, they switched jobs, and so on. Here are the questions to ask yourself:

1. Do I think positively about my writing and research tasks outside of my allotted research time?

2. Do I get excited when I think about my research projects or when I have new ideas?

3. Do I look forward to the research-related tasks on my to-do list and my calendar?

4. When possible, do I attempt to work on my research during unexpected free time?

5. Do I, or can I, accomplish other tasks of similar complexity and length, or have I done so in the past?

6. Do I find myself using skills to accomplish long projects that are not research related? If so, do I find these easy to accomplish?

7. Do I often push my research-related tasks to a different time or cancel them all together?

8. During my writing time, do I find myself wanting to engage in other more mundane tasks or becoming easily distracted?

If you answered yes to the first four questions, you may be struggling with a skill deficit, and the recommendations in this chapter specific to time management, as well as chapter 7, will be immensely helpful to you. If you answered yes to the second four questions, you may be struggling with a motivation issue, and the rest of this chapter will help you more clearly identify that and overcome it.

So let's begin to tackle the motivation issue. First, after you've set research goals for yourself, check in on them often. Are you forcing yourself to finish a project for another reason other than interest and enjoyment? Often, you can start with a strong interest in something, but for various reasons, you lose interest in it. Remember, this is okay! It's likely that nobody is forcing you to do this research, so if you aren't interested in it—don't do it!

Some of the reasons for losing interest may be that the findings thus far aren't that significant; after doing some research on the topic, you've identified another area you're more interested in; the effort required is much higher than you anticipated; or someone else conducted a similar study, minimizing the possible contribution of your project.

It may seem obvious to stop working on a project if you aren't interested in it anymore, but we often persist due to external influences, often even without our awareness. I have been in this situation several times during my career, and it wasn't until the past few years that I learned to recognize it and felt free enough to let go when I identified I wasn't interested any more. This often occurred when someone else had the idea and I jumped on it, or when a well-meaning colleague continued to "check in" on the project, leaving me to feel obligated to finish it. These circumstances can create a false sense of interest that, when removed, often diminishes. Be aware of these external influences and identify them as early as possible so you can change course when you want to.

That's not to say that you will find all parts of all projects interesting all the time. But, if the stress outweighs the fun, you may want to consider alternatives. Your options may include:

- Stop the research project all together.

- Consider whether other members of your research team or junior team members in your company may like to take that research over.

- Become the second or third author and let someone else take the lead.

- Take a break from the project and come back to it after a certain amount of time.

- Work on another project for a small amount of time and then come back to this one to see if anything has changed for you.

- Reframe the project based on recent literature to ensure you are asking and answering a relevant research question.

Once you've asked yourself these questions, reflect on your professional life and how research fits into it. Sounds existential, right? Kind of—but this type of reflection is useful at any point in your life when you hit a roadblock or face challenges to something you want to accomplish, or when a preferred activity becomes difficult or aversive. We are constantly growing and evolving as people, but also as a profession. Thus, it's necessary to assess your commitments, relationships, and work-life balance. Once you assess these parts of your life, you should adjust as necessary so you can continue to accomplish your goals and enjoy them while doing so!

On Self-Care and Balance

Behavior analysts are a hardworking crew! It is quite rare that I meet a behavior analyst who has figured out how to (or can!) work a 9 to 5 job, Monday through Friday, and avoid work in the evenings, on weekends, and on holidays while having good separation between their career and personal life. One look at our conference schedule throughout the year shows just how true this is—most conferences run through weekends, and commitments go late into the evenings—some even on holidays! We seem to have a "yes" culture in the name of "contributing to the field" that leads us to not only doing our full-time jobs but volunteering on "this" committee or sitting on "that" board, all to propel the field along.

This is not all bad—it means our services are needed, that many people are benefiting from our hard work and we are collectively making the world a better place through our amazing science! Where it becomes problematic is when this type of obsessive working around the clock, saying yes to everything, and volunteering our personal time gets in the way of the things we enjoy doing.

Remember in the introduction, when I told you that I changed positions, thinking I would never conduct research again? Part of that statement came from the fact that I was pretty burned out. I interpreted those feelings of burnout with my job as also burnout on the things I really enjoyed doing—including research. But when I assessed the reasons for not wanting to do research anymore, I found that it wasn't about research at all—it was about the space I worked in, the tasks I did every day, and the culture of my work environment. When those variables were removed, it turned out I really liked research. So much so that I was willing to do a lot of it on my own time and found the focus I needed to be quite productive!

If you are struggling to manage your time and be a productive researcher, take some time to look at your life, your job, and your goals. Ask yourself the following questions:

- Do I work a reasonable workday (knowing that some days may be longer than others, but overall, the time put in is reasonable)?

- Do I enjoy my work?

- Do I enjoy my colleagues?

- Do I have enough time to spend doing the leisure activities I enjoy that are not related to my profession?

- Am I sleeping well?

- Am I eating a well-balanced diet?

- Am I spending time with friends and family?

- Am I exercising?

- Am I spending time outdoors?

- Am I proud of my work?

If the answer to any (or all!) of these questions is no, you may need to make changes to your lifestyle, career, or commitments to make progress on your research. Do not be afraid to do so! Be selfish! Make time for yourself, have a career you truly enjoy, and make time for research if you want to do it. That may mean excusing yourself from other commitments to the field or saying no to future ones—but it's well worth it. I consider these types of contributions to be helpful earlier in one's career. They often help you network, learn about a new area of the field, and even ask applied research questions. However, it does not take years and dozens of commitments to reap these benefits, and over time you can fade them out to a reasonable number and time commitment.

I candidly remember the point in my career when I said no to a volunteer position for the first time. It was a pivotal moment for me—I realized that while I had said yes to everything that came my way, and that those yesses helped me learn a lot and make a name for myself in the field, they no longer served that function. Although I recognize that I always have something to learn, I realized that most people who asked me to volunteer would get more out of my involvement than I would. So I started saying no. Much to my delight, people were not upset as I thought they'd be. They understood. I always did so professionally and recommended someone else who might do the job well. And as I started saying no, it allowed me to have that extra time for research, which is where I wanted to spend my extra time. It also allowed me the opportunity to say yes to writing this book—a goal I've had for a long time and one that if I had other major commitments filling my time, I would not have been able to accomplish.

Over the course of the past four years, I've dwindled down my "extracurricular" activities to sitting on one board of directors and serving as an associate editor (AE) for one journal. These positions take up some time, but not so much that I don't have time to enjoy my full-time job and life. And importantly, I greatly enjoy both. I have a full-time job and a family—and I'm a researcher. Despite these roles, I do not feel overwhelmed. I feel perfectly fulfilled, grateful that I have the time to read, write, come up with new ideas, and live a healthy life. You will find your balance too—just open the door to change, saying yes only when you really want to and focusing on productivity as an applied researcher. In his book *Essentialism: The Disciplined Pursuit of Less*, Greg McKeown (2014) talks about being systematically disciplined in the way you evaluate every commitment, eliminating things in your life that are not absolutely essential. According to McKeown, this allows individuals to make their greatest contribution in life and focus on things that really matter. If research really matters to you, it may mean cutting out the nonessential things so you can make space for it without feeling overcommitted and overburdened.

Now that you've thought through the important issues of motivation, self-care, and life balance, let's focus on specific ways to improve your time management as a researcher.

Time-Management Strategies

Managing your time and staying productive with your research requires completing a task analysis, planning and scheduling, taking data and making data-based decisions, working on tasks in order, and focusing on one project at a time. All of these strategies are doable if you follow the suggestions below.

Complete a Task Analysis

As a behavior analyst, you know what a task analysis is and how to write one. You have an advantage here in that most of your daily activities likely involve breaking behaviors down into small chunks and tackling them one at a time to produce a full behavior chain. You likely create task analyses in the context of providing services to clients and, luckily, in your work on becoming an applied researcher.

For this strategy, I cannot emphasize enough that your steps should be *small* and *manageable*. I often talk to individuals who attempt to tackle lofty goals in one sitting, which only creates frustration, a feeling of lack of accomplishment, and ultimately an inclination to give up. I, too, made this mistake early in my research career, and while I managed to stay somewhat productive, the process and experience was not enjoyable, and I almost gave up. As an example, I would often set a goal to "write the introduction" of a certain paper and give myself three or four hours to accomplish this task. Or, I'd say something like "begin working on XXX paper."

There are several problems with these types of goals. First, they are much too vague. What exactly goes into writing an introduction? (Spoiler alert—a LOT of different behaviors, including brainstorming a "pitch" and rationale for my paper, conducting a literature search, reading relevant articles, narrowing down my search, creating an outline, and more). Several substeps are also needed to accomplish this entire task, which I haven't identified, let alone even done yet. Second, there are major issues with my allotted time. Very few people can sit down and work on one single task, uninterrupted, for a three- to four-hour chunk. Realistically, if you give yourself this amount of time (assuming you can find that much in your busy schedule), you're likely to work for twenty minutes, take a break, make a meal, check your email, daydream, get distracted on social media, work for another fifteen minutes, get frustrated that you haven't written the entire introduction yet, and call it a day. Given the negative experience you had, you may not schedule another research day until weeks or even months later. You can see how people quickly lose motivation and get very little, if anything, accomplished over the course of a year. You are much better off dedicating a small amount of *focused* time to discrete tasks. Even ten very focused minutes per day with the right task can be highly productive.

Remember, this is a marathon, not a sprint, so you'll be working on a project for several weeks, even months at time. The key here is consistency—daily goals and dedicated focus will get you further than infrequent sessions with lofty goals and fleeting focus. The task analysis will vary greatly depending on your chosen project, but here are a few examples.

Let's say I have an interest in a new topic and want to explore a possible study about training practices in the area of mandated reporting in our field. I've already identified this as a topic of interest, but I do not know much about what's out there—has any behavior analyst published on this topic? How about other disciplines? I need to start somewhere to put action behind this idea. My initial task analysis might look something like the following:

- Choose the most appropriate keywords to use in a literature search.

- Identify the search engines to use to conduct the literature search.

- Create a folder for storage of literature.

- Type chosen keywords into at least two search engines.

- Review titles of articles produced in the search for relevance; download and save them.

- Identify other search engines that may produce additional results.

- Type chosen keywords into remaining search engines.

- Review titles of articles produced in the search for relevance; download and save them.

- Read ____ articles (typically 1–2).

- Read ____ articles.

Or, let's say I've made it so far as to submit a paper for publication, and the decision is "reject with invitation to resubmit" (meaning they like the paper, but it needs substantial revisions and to go out for review to a new panel before making a final decision). Your task analysis might look something like this:

- Read and take notes on the letter from the AE.

- Read reviewer 1 comments.

- Read reviewer 2 comments.

- Read reviewer 3 comments.

- Read reviewer 4 comments.

- Make a list of all the changes that need to be made.

- Make ____ number of changes or edit ____ number of pages, continuing to work through the edits until complete.

- Reread the paper.

- Make final edits.

- Send to coauthor with deadline.

- Reread and edit.

- Check references.

- Submit paper.

Here is another example of a task analysis for developing a research topic—yes, this is something that can and should go on your to-do list and be broken down into small, manageable pieces:

- Sit down with a blank Word document and brainstorm.

- Add a few extra sentences or questions on one idea that is particularly interesting.

- Do a quick literature search using keywords to see what exists already.

- Read one article on the topic.

- Read a second article on the topic.

- Revisit your idea—confirming whether it is worth pursuing or not.

- Solidify your research question.

- Write the introduction and rationale of a protocol.

- Write the methods section.

- Create hypothetical graphs and results.

- Talk with colleagues about the possibilities for recruitment that exist.

Don't be afraid to create task analyses for other types of research-related tasks as well, such as speaking engagements or becoming informed about new practices in a specific area by reading recent research. As an example, if your paper is accepted to be presented at a local conference, your task analysis might look like this:

- Create an outline.

- Write an introduction.

- Write the ending.

- Write PowerPoint slides.

- Create matching visuals for PowerPoint slides.

- Practice the presentation.

- Refine and revise based on notes taken during the practice run.

- Practice again and time it.

- Practice in front of colleagues.

….you get the point. While this task may seem overly detailed, you'll need to do each of these steps to accomplish your bigger goal. Thus, writing them out, identifying certain times to accomplish them, and crossing them off your list will both make you feel accomplished and help you toward your goal. Depending on how much time you have, you could target more than one goal in a sitting—or simply be proud to accomplish one thing on your to-do list, even if it only took you seven minutes! Finally, do not hesitate to put small tasks on your task analysis, especially when you are first starting your research career. When I work with junior researchers, they often minimize the tasks they feel they need to accomplish, thinking they are not important enough to be considered research and to put on their task list. Examples include emailing someone to ask about a project, downloading an article they want to read, and reaching out to a colleague to schedule a brainstorming meeting. These are all absolutely important research tasks and you should put them in your task list! When someone on my team says, "I do not know where to start," I often say, "Yes you do." I encourage them to take ten minutes and a blank piece of paper and to write down everything they want to do to get started on research. I tell them to dismiss any interfering thoughts or doubts that what they want to accomplish is too little and just write. And you know what? They always come up with several tasks! You know what to do—you just need to consider it research, write it down, and plan to do it.

Take a few moments to create a task analysis for a project you are working on or an idea you want to develop. List the steps here:

_____

_____

_____

_____

_____

_____

_____

_____

_____

Plan and Schedule

This may be the most important strategy for becoming and remaining productive as an applied researcher: planning and scheduling. If you want to do research, you must both plan for it and schedule time to do it. If you have already completed a task analysis per the recommendations above, you have already started planning.

The process of listing every project you want to accomplish and completing a task analysis is imperative to your success. In fact, you should be a bit obsessive about it, especially at first. Review it daily, examining each project to confirm you have the steps laid out and your priorities are where you want them to be. It is okay to change your plan over time. For example, you may realize that a conference paper submission deadline is forthcoming and decide that finishing up a data-based project before the deadline is more important that starting a new literature review, so you move the conference paper submission up on the priority list. Or, you may discover that there are several additional substeps involved in a project and list those out as additional tasks to complete.

I keep my research/writing to-do list separate from my other to-do lists because this helps me compartmentalize the work and prevents me from becoming overwhelmed. The work on the research list is not work I'll be attempting to accomplish throughout the day—I will tackle it during my dedicated research time. However, I keep it as a simple Word document on my desktop and I look at it daily, sometimes even multiple times a day. This examination helps me stay grounded in the work that needs to be done and on my plans for my next writing session, and even for the next six months. It also gives me time to think about my tasks while I am not working on them, and I often consider how I'll tackle my next task, determine the order I will work in, or even come up with a new idea outside of my regular research time. I like to be very familiar with my to-do list—almost having it memorized so I can have these types of considerations anytime throughout the day.

The second part of this strategy, once you've adequately planned, is to schedule. This is crucial! You must find and dedicate time in your schedule for research, and *only* research. I enjoy the consistency of writing at the same time every day, and for me, that is first thing in the morning. I also try to write five days per week (Monday–Friday), even if just for ten minutes a day. This pattern helps me remember where I left off and keep momentum going, but also gives me a nice break on the weekend to refresh and look at my work with fresh eyes come Monday. I also typically schedule about an hour and a half, but I rarely use the full time. If I need it, it's there; if I don't, I get my day started. I focus on the tasks I accomplish during that time, not the amount of time spent.

Your schedule might look very different, and you should choose a frequency and duration that works for you. For some, spending a few hours on Saturday and a few on Sunday works quite well. For others, writing late at night a few days per week is the perfect arrangement. The actual schedule does not matter much, it is the fact that you have a schedule in place and stick to that schedule that is important.

Paul Silvia (2007), in his book *How to Write a Lot*, offers several strategies for academics wishing to write more. I read his book about halfway through my research career, and, while I've adapted some of his strategies and ideas to fit a behavior analytic conceptualization and my style of writing, one main takeaway from his book was the idea of consistent scheduling. I highly recommend you read this book (or at least the section on scheduling) for additional inspiration for creating and maintaining a schedule. This is important not just to research but to any project-based work or big initiative. Additionally, Cal Newport (2016) is a well-published author and has advocated for a strategy called "time blocking," wherein every minute of your day is accounted for—away from social media, the internet, and other distractions. Newport's idea is applied to all work you do every day. I implement time blocking for my entire workday, including my early morning writing time, and I find it highly effective. Read his book, *Deep Work: Rules for Focused Success in a Distracted World*. Even if you only apply scheduling and time blocking to your research tasks, you will be surprised at how your productivity soars! The theme here is to plan for specific writing time, schedule it, and commit to that scheduled time consistently.

Complete the following statements to establish a schedule that works for you:

1. I could conduct research with participants _____ days per week.

2. I will write/organize/plan for research _____ days per week.

3. I will write/organize/plan for research for _____ minutes at a time.

4. The days and times I will focus on research include:

    _____

    _____

Really think through your schedule. What will it be like to transition from one task to research and back? Will the transition be difficult? Have you accounted for basics like breaks, drive time, and meals? Is the time of day you've chosen ideal for you in terms of thinking and focusing? Are you likely to get too distracted by other tasks during your time and, if so, are there measures you can put in place to prevent distraction?

Once you've established a schedule, put the appointments on your calendar! Go ahead and do it—NOW!

Take Data and Make Data-Based Decisions

Collect data on your research and writing behavior, and if you find you are not meeting your goals or accomplishing as much as you'd like, like any good behavior analyst—make a change. If that change has an impact, stick to it. If it does not, make another change. For example, let's say you decide to get up very early in the morning and tackle your research list for one hour, five days per week. You find that you do well on this schedule for about the first week but then start missing some days by sleeping in or needing to do other things with that time. If skipping your research time goes on for several weeks (perhaps just days), it may be that you were too ambitious with your goal to get up that early every day. You might try reducing the number of days from five to three to see if your compliance increases. Or, you might try moving the schedule to start slightly later to see if that makes a difference. You should never go several days of missing your scheduled research time (unless you are sick or another specific life event gets in the way) without changing something.

Remember you are a behavior analyst and you can take effective data, analyze it, make changes, and assess each change to see what sort of impact it has on your own actions. Enter data on your research behavior and visually inspect it daily. I have played around with different data-collection techniques over the years. For me, a simple system of the date, session number, project I worked on, quick notes, and whether I met my daily goal or not (1 = yes, 0 = no) works very well. At the end of the month, I calculate the percentage of days with my goal met. I try to stay above 90%, and if I dip below that, I make a change. The visual is powerful. Sometimes I feel a bit guilty about not accomplishing my goal or missing a day, but when I look at the overall average of goal accomplishment, I am happy with the results. Below is a sample of my visual. Your data collection and visual inspection may be different. For example, you might analyze the number of projects completed over a period of months, or even the amount of time spent in research behavior. The important thing is to find a visual that works for you and use it.

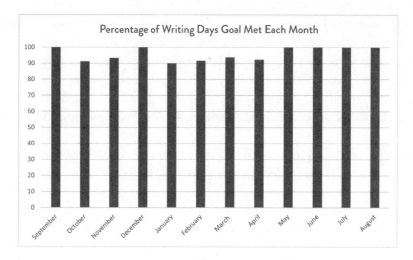

Visual depiction of my research and writing behavior. The X axis is months and the Y axis is the percentage of goals met. On average, during the year depicted, I met 96% of my writing goals.

Below, list the behaviors that are most important to you and how you want to graph them. Some examples include number of words written, number of pages written, number of new ideas developed, minutes spent on research, days spent on research, total duration of time spent on research.

Research behavior 1: _____

Research behavior 2: _____

Research behavior 3: _____

Research behavior 4: _____

Work on Tasks in Order

In a fast-paced world where we are all constantly doing more than one thing at a time and bouncing back and forth between tasks, it can seem counterintuitive to recommend that you work in order. However, this can be key to getting things done! There is a reason you created that task analysis, and there is a rhyme and reason to the sequence you put the tasks in. Following them in order will give you the ability to stay focused and to accomplish one thing before moving on to the next in chronological order. While skipping around on your list may not seem too detrimental for some tasks, take the following scenario.

Let's say you have on your list to finish reading a certain number of articles and then transition into writing your introduction. You probably created your task list that way because you knew that reading those articles first would result in a more robust and comprehensive introduction. Perhaps along the way in your reading, you get a little bored and decide to stop reading and write the introduction. Then, after you've finished, you bounce back to your reading and discover there are several key articles that change the message of your introduction. Of course, you can go back and rework it, but chances are you've wasted a bit of time by jumping the gun. So instead of jumping in to start your introduction if you find yourself getting bored with the reading, I recommend making notes to remind yourself of your ideas or taking a complete break from your reading task before going back to it. This will give you the refresher you need while not compromising your progress and jumping the gun.

Take some time to examine the task analysis you created above. Double check to ensure it is in a logical order. If you are feeling very ambitious, take each of those tasks and place them on your calendar as your mini goal for each writing session. Do this for about the first week—any further and you will be anticipating too far ahead of time how much you will be able to accomplish in each session and will likely need to change it anyway.

Focus on One Project at a Time

Bouncing back and forth between projects can disrupt your flow and stop momentum. Though it may be tempting to work on more than one project at once, avoid this to ensure optimal productivity. Plus, it can be very reinforcing to complete one project before moving on to the next. A product of the editorial process is that once you submit a paper for publication, you will have plenty of time to focus on the next project because you cannot work on the old one until you get a decision back. If you get distracted by a new project before submitting the first, you may never see the full one through to the end.

Take a few moments to list your projects. Ensure you have them all listed and put them in order of priority. Commit to tackling only one of them at a time before proceeding to the next. List your projects in order of priority here:

_____

_____

_____

_____

_____

Essential Takeaways

Effective time management strategies are crucial to becoming and remaining productive as an applied researcher. The strategies you implement must be specific to the task of conducting applied research. When you encounter difficulties with productivity, diagnose whether you are experiencing a skill deficit or a motivational deficit. Act according to your discovery. Remember to identify your own stress levels and ensure you are taking care of your basic health needs and have balance in your life. When you accomplish these things, you'll be ready to tackle creation of a task analysis, planning and scheduling, taking data on your own behavior, working on tasks in order, and completing one project at a time. Remember, there will likely never be an "ideal" time to get research done. You must commit to it, make the time, and then stick to your plan and work at your own pace. The strategies outlined in this chapter will help you maintain productivity over the course of your career as an applied researcher. Of course, there will still be roadblocks, and in the next chapter we'll explore several strategies for overcoming them.

CHAPTER 6

Overcoming Obstacles and Barriers

There are several obstacles and barriers that can interfere with your productivity as a researcher. For the purpose of this chapter, I use "obstacle" to refer to something that can easily be addressed by an individual, and "barrier" as an institutional blockage that's going to require the help (or at least cooperation) of others in order to find a work-around. The obstacles and barriers I'll address in this chapter were initially identified via a survey my colleague (Jessica Juanico) and I conducted that was completed by 834 professionals, mostly BCBAs. We reported the results in our paper that was published in *Behavior Analysis in Practice* (Valentino & Juanico, 2020). The survey asked participants to share information about the organizations for which they worked (e.g., whether they have opportunities for research, access to an IRB), their interest in research, and how much that interest influenced things like job choice and longevity with an organization.

We also asked about obstacles and barriers to accomplishing their research endeavors. The top five noted by respondents were lack of access to an IRB or RRC, lack of time, lack of mentorship, lack of opportunity, and lack of a research community. These five obstacles and barriers are so important that I've dedicated either parts of other chapters or entire chapters to overcoming them. In this chapter, I will address each of the remaining ones—lack of knowledge, fear of making a mistake, lack of research ideas, lack of opportunities, and limited or no access to literature—along with ways to overcome them.

Obstacles

It is common for practitioners to experience obstacles in their quest to conduct research. Obstacles are often related to one's own feelings and ideas about the task at hand. Luckily, obstacles can be easily overcome by engaging in specific actions. In this next section, I describe some of the most common obstacles practitioners face and actions you can take to overcome them.

Obstacle 1: Lack of Knowledge

Many of the respondents to our survey said that lack of knowledge was an obstacle they needed to overcome before attempting applied research. Some behavior analysts may feel they lack knowledge of experimental design and of research processes, which can inhibit their pursuits. It is true that some graduate programs may not emphasize this area sufficiently. You can relearn (or learn for the first time) with self-study and support.

I recommend going back to your primary textbooks and reading specific chapters related to single-subject design. Review your BCBA exam prep materials, but do so through the lens of conducting research. Ask yourself—if I had to do this tomorrow, what would I do? How would I use the information? Read and study the material like an applied researcher. My guess is that you read it differently before—as a student who needed certain information for a certain event or class. This time read it so you can *use* it. This different perspective should greatly facilitate your knowledge on the topic. By the very nature of having your BCBA, you have a foundation—you just need to brush up and apply the knowledge to a new and applied situation. This is not uncommon.

When I left graduate school and went into the work force, I had to brush up on several areas of study. For example, during graduate school, I studied the ethics code for mostly memorization purposes—I passed tests containing that information and knew some of the codes. But when I needed to *apply* the ethics code to a real-life situation that happened during practice, I froze and felt completely unknowledgeable. Brushing up on that material and thinking about it in the face of these real issues was immensely helpful in facilitating my knowledge and confidence.

Other behavior analysts may feel they have a lack of knowledge of the subject they want to study—for example, verbal behavior or organizational behavior management. When individuals talk about this as a deficit, it's often the conceptual part they're acknowledging a weakness in. This is also not uncommon, though I'd venture to say it's not as much of an obstacle as you might think. While you will need to have knowledge of the concepts behind your area of study, these are things you can look up, speak with your mentor about, attend conference talks related to, read other articles as models of, and generally reference whenever you want. If you set up your study with a strong conceptual foundation, you can incorporate those ideas into your discussion section when you write the paper, with any references you need by your side to do it correctly.

Here is a list of things you can do brush up on experimental design and specific content areas in behavior analysis. I do not recommend doing everything in each content area—there are costs associated with some of these actions. Choose an area of interest and commit to the action list in the area you'll be primarily researching to start.

Experimental Design

1. Review textbooks.

2. Review exam prep materials.

3. Review articles exemplifying different experimental designs.

4. To brush up on visual inspection skills, look at one phase of a data set at a time and practice describing the data in terms of trend, level, and variability. If you do this with a published article, "check" your work by reading the results section.

5. Make a hypothetical graph for your study, mapping out what an ideal data set would look like—one that demonstrates perfect experimental control.

Organizational Behavior Management

1. Subscribe to the *Journal of Organizational Behavior Management* (JOBM) (https://www.tandfonline.com/toc/worg20/current).

2. Join the Organizational Behavior Management (OBM) Network (http://obmnetwork.com/membership-benefits/) and begin receiving its newsletters.

Supervision

1. Subscribe to the journal *Behavior Analysis in Practice* (BAP) https://www.springer.com/journal/40617 (many supervision articles are published here).

2. Review the 2016 special issue on supervision in BAP.

Ethics

1. Join the Ethics and Behavior Analysis special interest group through ABAI (https://www.abainternational.org/constituents/special-interests/special-interest-groups.aspx).

2. Download the BACB's ethics code (http://www.bacb.com/wp-content/uploads/BACB-Compliance-Code-english_190318.pdf) and have it readily available.

3. Do a search in *Behavior Analysis in Practice* (BAP) (https://www.springer.com/journal/40617) and read some articles on ethics.

4. Purchase and review Bailey and Burch's *Ethics for Behavior Analysts*

Verbal Behavior

1. Subscribe to the journal *The Analysis of Verbal Behavior* (TAVB) (https://www.springer.com/journal/40616).

2. Join the Verbal Behavior Special Interest Group (VB-SIG) through ABAI and begin receiving its newsletters (https://www.abainternational.org/constituents/special-interests/special-interest-groups.aspx)

Problem Behavior

1. Read recent articles on problem behavior, focusing on specific areas of interest (e.g., automatically maintained problem behavior).

2. Connect with a problem behavior researcher to obtain mentorship.

3. If you do not have a case on your caseload where the focus is assessment and treatment of problem behavior, ask to have one assigned or shadow another clinician with this type of case.

Feeding

1. Join the special interest group Pediatric Feeding Disorders through ABAI.

2. Connect with a feeding researcher to obtain mentorship.

3. If you do not have a case on your caseload where the focus is assessment and treatment of feeding problems, ask to have one assigned (with supervision and support) or shadow another skilled clinician with this type of case.

Identify an area of weakness for yourself. Can you think of any other actions you could take to facilitate learning on this topic? List them here.

_____

_____

_____

_____

_____

_____

_____

Obstacle 2: Fear of Making a Mistake

I can appreciate this obstacle! I too, had many fears of making a mistake when conducting research and constantly second-guessed myself. Overcoming this obstacle involves changing your thinking about research, what it means to publish, and how you do it. It was not until later in my research career that I realized that making mistakes is a critical part of the research process. Making mistakes helps you answer questions, steers your ideas in the right direction, and often makes a valuable contribution to the field.

As an example, in the study I discussed earlier on menstrual care by Veazey et al. (2016), several changes to the clinical protocol needed to be made for one of the participants. Specifically, after several trials of the forward chaining procedure, one participant continued to err on proper use of a sanitary napkin. As such, the clinicians systematically added steps to the chaining procedure to address and correct this error. These changes were not applied to the other participant but changed the independent variable for one participant. The research team could have viewed these changes as "mistakes" or as confusing the experimental design. Instead, they chose to embrace them and discuss why they were important to the effectiveness of the intervention, demonstrating how to solve a clinical problem when it occurs while maintaining treatment integrity and demonstrating experimental control.

I highly recommend this embracing and reconceptualizing these "mistakes" as "changes." Also, ask yourself, *What's the worst that could happen here?* So what if you make a mistake? When you assess the worst-case scenario, you'll probably find it's not so bad! You may have to ditch the data set or do more writing to explain the change of events, but these things are not at all problematic and will result in a better experience and a better contribution. So, go on! Make mistakes—and be proud of them!

Here are some questions you can ask and answer to support you in overcoming fear of making mistakes:

1. Do I have a real deficit in this area or is it just fear?

2. If I do have a deficit, what are two or three simple things I could do to acquire the skill?

3. If I proceed with conducting research today, what is the worst thing that could happen?

4. Have I made clinical mistakes in the past? If so, what have I learned from them?

5. Can I identify one person I admire who made a mistake? How did they respond to it?

6. When I start to feel fearful in the future, what is one thing I can do to help calm myself and stay focused?

Here are some sample responses to those questions:

1. Do I have a real deficit in this area or is it just fear?

    I think it is mostly just fear. I have a solid academic background in experimental design. While I may need to brush up on some of those skills, I have the knowledge. I think I am just scaring myself into thinking something could go wrong that would jeopardize my career.

2. If I do have a deficit, what are two to three simple things I could do to acquire the skill?

    I could review some chapters from my Cooper text on experimental design, read a research article that utilizes a design I'm considering using, and talk to my supervisor about a study I just read that I want to use as a rationale for my new study.

3. If I proceed with conducting research today, what is the worst thing that could happen?

    Nothing really! If I make a mistake, I can start over, or use that mistake in a way that helps me tell a story about the data I obtain. I always know what to do clinically to correct a problem, so I will know what to do with research.

4. Have I made clinical mistakes in the past? If so, what have I learned from them?

I have made clinical mistakes in the past, of course! I remember one time I interpreted parts of the Verbal Behavior Milestones Assessment and Placement Program (VBMAPP), a common assessment and curriculum guide used with individuals with autism, incorrectly for a client. I started implementing some programming that was far too advanced for him. I learned that even a mistake like that can yield some good results! Surprisingly, he actually learned some of those higher-level skills, which changed the way I programmed for him and allowed him to make faster progress. This is a mistake I would repeat if I could! It was so beneficial! I suppose any mistakes I make in research have the potential to have the same positive influence.

5. Can I identify one person I admire who made a mistake? How did they respond to it?

Yes! My advisor in graduate school is someone I admire very much. She made a mistake in development of a research consent form. Once she identified it, she acted with a high degree of integrity. She corrected the mistake, contacted the participants in the study, notified the IRB, and took action to ensure no harm was done. If I make a mistake, I will follow this example of acting with integrity, for sure!

6. When I start to feel fearful in the future, what are some things I can do to help calm myself and stay focused?

Remind myself that making a mistake will not have devastating consequences. Think of people in my life who have made mistakes and how they responded. Consider clinical mistakes I've made that actually benefited me and my clients. Remind myself to proceed without fear!

Obstacle 3: Lack of Research Ideas

It can be common, especially when you are new to research, to wonder what you want to study. I provide several recommendations in chapter 7 about how to overcome this obstacle. Keep in mind that once you decide to be a researcher, you should read more…and you should pay attention. Doing these two things is likely to lead to ideas. When you view your clinical work in the context of applied research questions, it's hard not to come up with new ideas. When you read articles about topics you are interested in, the authors often give you the ideas!

Also, utilize conferences and other continuing education events to the fullest! Take notes when you attend talks and write down all the new ideas you can think of based on the presenter's work—this is how I developed many of my research ideas, especially early in my career. Here is a to-do list for generating research ideas:

- Read articles on topics you are interested in. Generate ideas based on the discussion section or based on questions you have as you read through the article. Think freely during this phase—meaning don't question whether you are asking the right thing or not. Just be curious—*What about this? Why didn't they do that? What about kids who…?*

- Attend talks at conferences on topics you could potentially study. Write down all the "future directions" the author mentions and any ideas you have as you listen to the talk.

- Attend CEU events virtually or locally. Take notes on ideas and extension of current research on a topical area.

- Talk to other researchers about their ideas—don't steal them of course, but use them as motivation and an example of how to formulate your own thoughts.

- Take every opportunity to write down ideas—sometimes your best ideas come to you right before you go to bed, or while you are cooking breakfast. If you don't make a quick note, you might forget!

- Pay attention to the issues that present during your clinical care of clients.

- Ask your team about issues they are encountering in their clinical work—they may not yet have the skills to formulate those issues into a research question, but you do!

Barriers

As a reminder, unlike an obstacle, which can easily be addressed by an individual, a barrier is an institutional blockage that's going to require the help (or at least cooperation) of others in order to find a work-around. In this section, we will talk about common barriers. While navigating barriers will require some coordination with others and additional support, these too can be overcome if they are identified and an action plan is put in place to navigate them successfully. Two of the most common barriers include lack of opportunities and limited access to literature. I discuss these both in detail below.

Barrier 1: Lack of Opportunities

This is a real barrier and one that may be inherent in the organization where you work. It is, however, a barrier you can indeed overcome. The key to overcoming it is to create your own opportunities. It's highly unlikely someone will be sitting around ready to give you an idea, or have you collect data on a project that already exists. So, you should become that person. You may need to start small—talking to leaders in your organization about research, beginning to build infrastructure, chatting with a researcher in the field whom you admire, or reading articles. Starting with these small steps will help open the door to opportunities that will likely last long into the future to support your interests. Here is a to-do list to actively gain opportunities for research.

- Follow the steps in this book to establish a research infrastructure at your organization.

- Email someone who presented a unique study at a conference you attended. Ask them if they have any volunteer opportunities available for you to gain research experience.

- Develop a small project you could pursue with one client on your caseload.

- Read literature on a topic of interest.

Barrier 2: Limited Access to Literature

Carr and Briggs (2010) published a paper on strategies for making regular contact with the scholarly literature. In that paper, they discussed several barriers that can interfere with the ability to access literature and provided strategies on how to overcome them. They discussed these barriers in the context of our obligation to read the literature, which applies to those wanting to conduct research in applied settings as well. Their discussion is divided into three main barriers: searching the literature, accessing journal content, and contacting the contemporary literature. Below, I summarize their suggestions and then add some additional categories for you to consider.

- **Searching the literature**—Purchase individual or organizational subscriptions to PsychINFO, obtain PsychINFO access via an alumni association membership, deduct PsychINFO expenses on your tax return (Carr and Briggs, 2010).

- **Accessing journal content**—Follow inexpensive or free journals when possible, access archived articles in PubMed Central, obtain library access via alumni association membership, contact authors for reprints, use Google Scholar to locate electronic articles (Carr and Briggs, 2010).

- **Making contact with the contemporary literature**—Organize bookmarks to journal sites in your web browser, visit journal pages to review in-press articles, request table of contents email alerts, use Google Reader to monitor updates to journal websites, create a supportive social community, implement self-management procedures (Carr and Briggs, 2010).

In my experience, accessing journal content is a major barrier faced by practitioners. During graduate school, students have access to the university's resources, which allows them to access virtually any article, journal, or set of journals they wish, for free. This unlimited access encourages mental stimulation, supports research projects and study, provides a foundation for theses and dissertations, and creates a research culture inherent in the graduate school experience. Once a student graduates, that access abruptly stops. Access to the variety and type of literature one needs to maintain a research agenda post graduate school is costly and cumbersome.

Although journal subscriptions can be relatively inexpensive, a practitioner would need to subscribe to multiple journals to access literature on even just one topic—one journal would not suffice. While there are work-arounds to access search engines such as PsychINFO at a reduced rate, it still comes at an expense to the individual practitioner. So, practitioners can become quickly disconnected from the literature. This is common in all fields, not just behavior analysis—but may be even more pronounced given our profession's reliance on data and empirically validated treatments. Even if research is not a goal, practitioners have an obligation to implement strategies based on the literature and to stay current—which can feel impossible. In my many years working with practitioners, I have rarely met one who does not wish to read the literature. There is a strong desire among our BCBAs to access literature, read it, and contribute to it. My recommendation for solving this problem is to create a literature request system within your organization.

COMPANY-WIDE LITERATURE REQUEST SYSTEM

Consider setting up a literature request system at your organization—it's easier than you might think. At my current organization (TBH), we have established a cost-effective, efficient system that has worked quite well to give our clinicians (and anyone in the company) access to the research literature. We call it, simply, "the literature request system" (creative, I know!) and it utilizes our company intranet to host a webform that anyone can complete to request literature. You do not have to set up your system this way; to create a system yourself, you simply need access to literature and a way for individuals to request that literature from you or the research team. Let me explain an easy way to set up a literature request system.

First, your organization will need to invest in individual subscriptions to various journals and search databases, such as PsychINFO. This is a unique system that not only benefits individuals with regard to their research, but also helps them be better practitioners by staying in contact with the literature.

Next, you'll need to set up a way for people to request literature. To do this, follow these steps:

1. **Decide who will serve on the literature search team.** This, of course, could be you. It could be a group of volunteers and/or leaders in the organization who are interested in participating. Start by explaining the system to individuals in your organization and asking for volunteers. If certain people have already expressed interest in research, you can reach out to them directly to see if they'd like to be a part of the group. Of course, you'll want to request leadership's approval for those individuals to contribute some time to the task.

2. **Decide who will be the leader on the team.** You may need to have a conversation with your organization's leadership on this issue. Depending on the size of your organization, this job could take up a few minutes per month or a few hours per month. If you are the leader, you'll want to ensure your organization is supportive of your committing some time to this task. If someone else has taken the role on, you

can support leaderships' understanding of the role and also ensure the person can commit time to the task. The job will require the leader to ensure that all requests get responses in a reasonable amount of time (e.g., one week from time of submission).

3. **Identify a way literature requests will come to you.**

    a. If you have a team intranet, a simple webform can be utilized.

    b. If you do not have a team intranet, your IT (information technology) support could set up a simple email address, such as literaturerequest@ABAClub.com. While you won't be able to have fields, you can email the person for clarification as needed or set up a Word document that they must complete and send via email with specific fields for them to complete.

4. **Map out the information you and the research team need to complete the request.** I recommend including basic demographic information (name, title, position), the reason they are seeking literature (personal interest, for support with a case), and specific information that will help you locate the literature. If it is a specific article, simply ask them for the citation. If it is a group of articles, ask them for key terms and have them describe a bit about what they are looking for.

5. **Create the submission form.** If you decide to complete this via email, the information could simply be in a Word document or email template that you email to people to ensure you get the information you need from them to complete the search. If the form is through the intranet, work with your IT department to get it added to the company's page.

6. **Test the system.** Have a volunteer complete the form or send the email. Does it come through properly? Does the information you receive allow you to adequately find relevant literature that is helpful to the individual? Adapt your system after this pilot test to ensure you get the information you need in the format that is most conducive to efficient searching of the literature.

7. **Create a system for tracking the requests.** This should include information you'd like to know, such as type of request or response time of team. This tracking could be as simple as an Excel spreadsheet or Word document.

8. **Subscribe to the search engine PsychINFO.**

9. **Subscribe to various journals as needed.** I recommend *Behavior Analysis in Practice, The Analysis of Verbal Behavior,* and the *Journal of Applied Behavior Analysis* to start.

10. **Communicate to the organization about the resource.** Create an email or flyer to share the new resource with your organization. You might consider working with marketing, specifically those focusing on internal marketing, to help you create

something that articulates that this is a resource for team members, a perk of working for the organization.

11. **Tweak the forms and system as new needs arise.** You probably won't get everything right the first time, but that's okay! Tweak your system, communication, and forms as you identify gaps. These systems are very simple, so maintenance and changes should be straightforward and fast to make over time.

Note that around 2016, the Behavior Analyst Certification Board (BACB) provided all certificants with access to ProQuest through their online portal. This access makes it easier to access literature and is available for free if you remain an active certificant. Interestingly, even after this service was made available, the requests at my organization, TBH, continued to grow. I believe this is because many BCBAs struggle with how to effectively search the literature and, although they have access, may not know exactly how to get the articles they need. This leads us to our next topic.

How to Search the Literature

Before concluding this chapter, I want to spend some time providing information about how to effectively search the literature. This can be tricky, as search engines are often very sensitive. Here are some steps to follow.

Step 1: Get organized (Identify the following)

- Keywords

- Target behavior

- Specific interventions

- Demographic

- Relevant journals

- Access to journals

Step 2: Search

- Specific journals

- ProQuest

- PubMed Central

- References

- Google Scholar

STEP 3: Improve the search

- Change keywords, if necessary

- Check other journals

- Discover other interventions for target behaviors

- Can't find target population? Identify research with a different population

In addition to following these steps, remember to examine the array of resources you have available to you. These include:

- Behavior Analyst Certification Board (BACB) portal

- Google Scholar

- ResearchGate

- Specific journal search engines (e.g., JABA)

- Your organization's research request support

Here are some of the steps I might take for a specific search. Let's say I am interested in learning whether there is a difference in acquisition if I teach a kid to mand (request) using sign language or pictures. My answers and actions are below in *italics*.

Step 1: Get organized (Identify the following)

- Keywords—*pictures, sign language, manding, alternative communication*

- Target behavior—*manding*

- Specific interventions—*the Picture Exchange Communication System (PECS)*

- Demographic—*I am interested in the topic generally but need to know for my clients in the age range of three to five years old.*

- Relevant journals—*The Analysis of Verbal Behavior, Behavior Analysis in Practice, Journal of Applied Behavior Analysis*

- Access to journals—*I have access to all three of these journals.*

Next, I conduct step 2 (Search) using the organizational checklist in step 1. However, I realize I am not finding as much literature as I think there is on this topic, so I work to improve my search using step 3.

Step 2: Improve Search

- Change keywords, if necessary—*After a little digging, I realize there is some conceptual literature on this topic that discusses these systems in terms of selection-based verbal behavior and topography-based verbal behavior, so I decide to add these key terms into my search.*

- Check other journals—*I decide to expand my search to educational journals, speech journals, and more general behavioral journals to see what I can find there. I find a small line of literature on this topic in the journal* Education and Treatment of Children.

- Discover other interventions for target behaviors—*I learn there is broader literature in the alternative communication systems literature base that may be relevant, which includes use of technology such as tablets and voice output devices (VOCAS), so I decide to expand my question (and literature search) to be inclusive of these systems.*

- Can't find target population? Identify research with a different population—*N/A. I was able to find literature for my target population.*

This is a simple example of how I would think through a question and conduct a literature review according to my needs. Take a few moments to complete each of these steps on a topic of interest. If you do not yet have access to journals, complete the exercise in writing and save it for when you do have access. Often, the keywords and way you search will be shaped by what literature pops up when you do your initial search. The exercise is helpful to do even outside of the search engines so you can become accustomed to thinking about the type of literature you'd like to find.

I want to provide you with one additional resource to assist you in accessing literature. Due to an increased interest in connecting with the literature and the known barriers to doing so faced by practitioners, some organizations have developed resources that can be utilized for free or a small fee. If setting up a system within your organization is not possible, utilizing these services could be quite feasible. One such company is The PartnerShip, LLC. (https://www.baresearchcitations.com/). This company provides a service that "collates the latest research related to practicing behavior analysts." The literature is searched extensively, and you receive a list called "Contents," which includes basic information on new literature, a link to each article, and a summary. You can purchase an annual subscription that gives you access to the latest articles published every month and provides help finding full-text versions when available.

Essential Takeaways

This chapter has provided you with practical actions you can take to overcome common obstacles and barriers associated with conducting applied research. To overcome the obstacles, you'll have the opportunity to implement many of these strategies independently to support your knowledge, thinking, and idea generating. In the face of barriers, you'll work with other individuals to help create systems to overcome them. Identifying your own personal obstacles and the institutional barriers you face will facilitate fast progress toward your goal to become an applied researcher. Next we'll turn to other practical strategies that will help you achieve your goal.

Practical Strategies

There are several practical strategies that you can use to be successful in conducting research. Each of these strategies involves preplanning, not unlike other projects you have likely tackled in your career thus far—conducting a master's thesis, writing a term paper, even applying to graduate schools. In this chapter, I describe each of these practical strategies and offer ideas about how to incorporate them into your life so that you can begin, and succeed in, your career as an applied researcher.

Strategy 1: Make Decisions

While this may seem like an obvious first step, it is one that is often overlooked. If overlooked, your journey can start off in a way that creates confusion and quick burnout. There are several early decisions you'll need to make to begin conducting applied research. We'll address two here: why and what you want to research.

First, ask yourself, *Why do I want to conduct research?* Identify your motivators. Behavior analysts conduct research for lots of different reasons. Certain contingencies come in to play; for example, professors in university settings may need to publish a certain number of articles per year to be eligible for tenure, or a researcher may have a systematic line of existing research they want to continue to explore. As a practitioner, it is unlikely that your place of employment or immediate professional community imposes rules about writing, researching, and publishing. So you can identify your own motivators. Perhaps you simply want to contribute to the field of behavior analysis. Or maybe you want to grow professionally and challenge yourself, and research provides a clear path for you to do so. It can also be fun to develop a professional identity and research reputation—people recognize your name from work that you've published or presented at a conference. Each of these reasons is perfect, and the most important thing is that you find *your* personal, unique motivators and allow them to drive your research behavior.

The next important decision to make is *what* you want to research. This can certainly change over time as you tackle different projects and find out what you are passionate about, but you will need to make an initial decision about what you'd like your first project to be. In behavior analysis, there are several options: literature reviews, treatment models, recommended practice guidelines, or data-based research studies and within these categories, a myriad of topics to choose from. As you advance in your career as a researcher, you may find yourself serving as a reviewer on other papers and/or presenting at conferences. Each of these activities will require a different set of tasks, so identifying your first project will enable you to take very concrete steps toward your goal of becoming a researcher. There is no right answer here, except that your choice should be something that motivates and interests *you*. Much like choosing a dissertation or thesis topic, if you pick something you have very little interest in, you are likely to quit early in the process. It is also okay if these interests change over time.

Early in my career, I published mostly on the topic of verbal behavior—most of my papers were data-based studies and focused on identifying creative ways to establish verbal behavior repertoires in children with autism. I loved this part of my research career, and that line of research was quite conducive to my work environment at the time. However, over time, as my work environment and scope of job responsibilities changed, I became interested in broader topics. At first, these interests still involved individuals with autism, but not specifically focused on verbal behavior. I became very interested in strategies to teach unique adaptive skills to different profiles of learners and pursued several projects along these lines. Then I became interested in professional practice issues such as supervision, ethics, public speaking, and the topic of this book, applied research in clinical settings.

If I had forced myself to continue publishing in verbal behavior, I would not have been very productive or happy. I still conduct a study or two on verbal behavior every year, but this is mainly out of support of students or post docs rather than my own personal interest. I allowed myself flexibility in the topics I chose and let my motivators and interests guide my research behavior. Due to that flexibility and motivation, I get excited to write, present, and publish and am consistently eager to work those activities into my daily life. I assess my motivation regularly to see if I should change gears or continue on my current path. I anticipate I'll shift focus as I have done a few times throughout my career based on my work environment, modern literature, my opportunities, and my general interests.

Take a few moments and list the motivators you have for conducting research here. That is, answer the question: Why do I want to conduct research?

_____

_____

_____

_____

_____

_____

_____

Now answer the question: What do I want to research? It is okay to be general and broad right now (e.g., verbal behavior acquisition). You can get more specific as you start to identify questions and target populations for your work.

_____

_____

_____

_____

Strategy 2: Identify Research Questions Through Your Clinical Work

As you make these decisions, you'll have a clear path forward for creating your new identity as a practitioner-researcher. This can be exciting, and you'll likely start to encounter barriers, some related to time. You should always use the work you're already doing as a backdrop for your research. This could be in the form of identifying a clinical question with your clients (e.g., comparison of a few different prompting strategies, the need for a unique protocol to address a specific clinical issue) or an issue within your work setting (e.g., lack of a specific resource for supervision, collection of data on practical issues). Using the time you already have instead of carving out separate time will increase the likelihood of success. Most practitioners do not realize that there are research questions in front of them every day. Your job is to find and ask them and continue down the path of systematic questioning and answering.

Here are some things you can do to identify research questions through your clinical work:

- Carry a notebook or other means of taking notes with you and jot down ideas when you are providing services. What does the client struggle with?

- Ask your team members who work with your clients what they see. What areas need development?

- When you read research articles, think of specific clients who present similarly to those described in the study. Could you replicate that author's study or expand upon it in some way?

- Try out different procedures when working with your clients. Do you see promise in any of them? Are they novel and do they pose an opportunity for evaluation?

Strategy 3: Read

In order to write well, you must read. Reading provides models for how other people write, use words, and structure their sentences. Technical writing in the field of ABA is unique and may not come naturally to someone new to the research world. Spend time reading the work of good writers and of authors who publish on topics of interest to you. This will not only provide a model for how to write but will educate you on your topic of interest so you have a foundation to ask those questions and begin writing.

Identify and list three researchers whom you admire and who write well. Find an article they've written and plan to read it as part of your early research preparation work.

_____

_____

_____

Strategy 4: Create an Environment Conducive to Productivity

This strategy applies to writing and other work you will do independently on your research project. For data-based studies, it will apply at the beginning, during your planning stages, and at the end, during your writing stages. For other types of work (e.g., literature reviews, discussion papers), it applies to all steps in the process. It is imperative that you create stimulus control over your writing behavior. This involves choosing a place, a time, and specific stimuli you will have in your environment that will control your writing behavior. If possible, try to write at the same time every day (or every writing session) and in the same place. For me, this is first thing in the morning at my desk at home before my young son wakes up. I avoid allowing distractions into the environment or for my mind to shift to other activities. I wake up, pour a cup of coffee, go to my desk, and begin my task. I resist the urge to open emails, check my phone, or engage in other household tasks that would get in the way of my productivity. I have always set my goal the day before, so I consistently know what I'll be accomplishing during my writing time. Setting the goal ahead of time also gives me about twenty-four hours to think about how I want to approach my task, so when I sit down to write I always have ideas and a good framework for how I will tackle that day's goal. I never force myself to write outside of my writing time, but because I know what I want to accomplish, I sometimes have ideas throughout the day that I will jot down or take mental note of in order to best prepare for my next writing session. I also clear my desk of other distracting items that do not have anything to do with my writing session and ensure my own comfort (e.g., window open if it is cool outside, dimmer lights). The way you arrange your environment is very individualized, and you should pick what is best for you. Some people work best in other settings (e.g., coffee shops), with music playing, at their office before their workday starts, or after it ends. The critical activity is to remove distractions. You must resist the urge to check email or social media, do your dishes, and so on. Engaging in these other tasks will either distract you too much to focus on your writing or take up all your writing time. Here is a worksheet you can complete to identify basic elements of your environment that will be most conducive to research behavior. You can also download this worksheet at http://www.newharbinger.com/47827.

Research Environment Worksheet

Use this worksheet to identify the elements of your environment that will be most conductive to research behavior.

1. I am best able to concentrate when:

    a.   There is no noise in my environment

    b.   There is some noise in my environment (e.g., white noise, soft music)

    c.   There is a lot of noise in my environment (e.g., people talking, cars driving by, cash register dinging)

2. The temperature in my environment that makes me feel most comfortable is:

    a.   Very cold

    b.   Cool, but comfortable

    c.   Warm

    d.   Hot

3. The position in which I work best is:

    a.   Lying back, with my laptop on my lap

    b.   Sitting up at a desk with my materials on the desk

    c.   Sitting up on a couch with my laptop on my lap

    d.   Other (Describe)_____

4. The lighting in my environment that is most conducive to my productivity is:

    a.   Dim lighting from a lamp

    b.   Brighter lighting from a light in the room

    c.   Very bright lighting, fluorescent

5. Below, identify any stimuli that make you feel calm and focused. Examples might include motivating books or phrases, a notebook, different writing utensils or electronic tools, and office supplies such as sticky notes.

    _____

    _____

    _____

    _____

    _____

Strategy 5: Embed High-Quality Research Practices into Your Clinical Work

This strategy may take a little time to implement, but doing so will not only set you up to conduct research during your clinical work but will also improve the quality of your clinical work. The list below includes strategies to assist you in embedding research practices into your clinical work that will make conducting research easier.

1. Arrange for observers to conduct overlapping sessions during which the observers collect interobserver agreement (IOA) and treatment integrity (TI).

2. Train individuals working on specific cases to appropriately collect IOA and TI.

3. Have regular contact with your data so you can make decisions about phase changes and tweaks to the protocol.

4. Have clearly written protocols and procedures prior to implementing an intervention.

5. Track (and have team members) track every change you make to the protocol.

6. Only make one change at a time.

7. Control the targets or behaviors that are introduced according to your research design.

8. Provide education about research ethics to any individuals who will be working on a research project.

Strategy 6: Master the Art of Imperfection

Often, one's only experience in publishing is through a master's thesis or capstone project. These projects are intentionally designed to have very few flaws. You often have time to complete an extra data set or even to rethink your research design or question. Applied research is very different and requires you to become flexible and comfortable with imperfection. You or a team member collecting your data may decide to change phases at the "wrong" time, you may have many incomplete data sets, or one of your conditions may be confounded by a parent conducting trials outside of your sessions. All these things are inevitable in clinical practice. They should either be embraced and used to help you tell a different story about your data or they should encourage you to move on to a new participant or even a new research question. It is always refreshing to read a research article that acknowledges that something occurred in the participant's life or a change was made unexpectedly. Unfortunately, many authors choose to exclude these data sets or ignore the event altogether. This leads the reader to think that the conditions under which the study occurred were perfect, which then leads to others thinking the work may not apply to them in the often-messy clinical world or that they could never repeat a similar procedure in their everyday practice. Some research absolutely requires this level of control—translational and conceptual studies should be clean, and all variables should be controlled for when possible. However, applied research does not give that level of control. So, applied researchers must embrace variability, discuss change, and conceptualize breaks from the protocol in a way that is useful for their audience—this is applied research at its finest!

Strategy 7: Contact the Contingencies for Conducting Research

Earlier in this process, you identified your motivators. Hopefully, the contingencies for conducting research connect to those motivators. Much of this chapter has discussed publication as being the final contingency for applied research. However, there are many ways to contact other contingencies, and especially early in your research career, you should try to contact as many of those contingencies as frequently as possible. For example, you could submit your project to a conference as a poster or symposium. This will help you share your work with others, will be a line on your resume or curriculum vitae (CV) to share your professional growth and contribution with others, and likely will be an exciting event for you. You might also ask to share your projects with others in your organization, perhaps during a group supervision session for budding behavior analysts or at a company meeting. These smaller goals will allow you to contact social reinforcement for engaging in your work and give you opportunities to practice preparing your work for other avenues, such as publication.

Set three goals for yourself for this year that will help you contact the contingencies for conducting research. List them here:

_____

_____

_____

Strategy 8: Be Willing to Persist and be Patient

Applied research will present many challenges during every step of the process. When conducting data-based studies, you may not demonstrate experimental control; participants may stop services, leaving the study prematurely; or the question may not be of clinical relevance anymore. If working on a non-data-based study, you might find it difficult to locate articles that you need to "tell your story," realize someone has already published on that topic after you are halfway through writing the paper, or simply hit a roadblock regarding the direction you want to take.

Once you begin the editorial process, your willingness to persist is even more important, because, as I'll discuss in chapter 10, the editorial process can be quite long—years even. You should know ahead of time that your paper may get rejected (from multiple journals), it may get rejected but invited for a resubmission if you are willing to make substantial changes, and you may need to wait upward of three years before you see it in press. (In one situation, for a journal that was published infrequently, and working with an AE who was slow and required substantial and multiple revisions, I waited five years from the time of first submission to seeing it in press!) In a world where immediate gratification is not only common but expected, it can be extremely difficult to persist with a research agenda. I've met plenty of very ambitious and excited behavior analysts who want to get into research. They start off strong, have great ideas, and even submit them for publication! Then they receive a "revise and resubmit" decision or a "reject" from one journal, a long time after submission, and get discouraged. Many give up. So, you must prepare yourself to wait long periods of time for an outcome and—be patient. A colleague of mine once told me that conducting research is a test of how resistant your behavior is to extinction—this is certainly true!

You must be willing to persist through these roadblocks and keep trying. Having multiple projects going at the same time can help—for example, after you've submitted one paper for publication, you can start working on another one while you wait. Additionally, breaking everything into small steps is extremely helpful. For example, let's say a paper you submitted was rejected but the AE invited you to resubmit it. Your first task analysis step may be to simply read the AE letter. The next goal for the next writing session may be to read reviewer 1 comments, then to read reviewer 2 comments, and so on. Once you've gotten through reading, you might make goals to address a certain number of the AE's concerns (e.g., address issues 1 and 2). Before you know it, you've addressed all the changes and are ready for resubmission. The most important message here is to not give up. You must keep at it or your work will never be seen by anybody but you.

Strategy 9: Expand Your Research Opportunities

The more open you are to varied research ideas, projects, and involvement, the more opportunities you will have. For example, you may have never considered that you'd be interested in writing a literature review—but if you find a topic you are passionate about, this could be a great avenue for publishing. Perhaps you thought you'd just conduct research on verbal behavior topics with young children, but you identify a staff performance issue and dive into the organizational behavior management literature to get a study off the ground. Or perhaps someone offers you an opportunity to collect data on a project so you jump on it. This occurred with me upon transition to a new company. I did not yet have any of my own research projects, and a collaborator at a nearby university was finishing up data collection on her dissertation. In exchange for collaboration and my collecting data on one participant, I earned last author on the publication. Although I already had several of my own first author publications, this was a unique and well-timed opportunity for me. I learned a lot through collaborating with her and it was refreshing to be a data collector on someone else's study rather than leading everything! Collaborating with other professionals, such as those in human resources, recruiting, and even finance, could also prove helpful to your research endeavors. Applying behavior analytic strategies and experimental design to programs or new policies will not only help the organization evaluate effectiveness, but could make a very interesting and unique contribution to the field. You might consider publishing in other areas, such as psychology, counseling, or even business. Also consider being a third or fourth author on a paper someone else is leading—to learn and contribute without the pressure of doing it all.

Strategy 10: Become a Good Public Speaker

It may seem odd that a strategy I'm recommending for you to become good at doing research is to become a good (or great!) public speaker. Public speaking can do a lot for you in terms of your research agenda. First and foremost, it can give you the opportunity to share your ideas with others. This connection—through conferences, conventions, state association meetings, or even local meetup groups—can expand your opportunities to collaborate with and obtain input from colleagues on your work and ideas. In addition, you may have some projects that never get published in the traditional sense but that you'll present several times in your career that will absolutely make contributions to the field.

One study comes to mind for me—an applied piece of work with an older man with autism. This man had not walked in over two years—he crawled around his home and, at the time we intervened, was even refusing to get up to go to the bathroom and use the toilet, even though he had been fully toilet trained since he was very young. There was no medical explanation for his lack of walking—it was purely behavioral. During our time with him, my team and I used simple shaping and chaining to get him to walk again. We broke every task down into very small, manageable steps and targeted them one at a time. At the end of intervention, we had put over 1,000 sessions in, but he was walking independently around the house! I have videos from the first days of treatment, where we were struggling to get him up off the floor, to the last day, where he is walking with only a light touch from his caregiver—it's truly incredible to watch. I've presented this data in different forums over the years and each time I have had a round of applause after people see the video. They are inspired and often reminded why our science is so powerful. I don't think this case study will ever make it to press. It's not because it is not good—it's just that we used some pretty basic procedures and the graphs just don't paint the picture in the way my voice paired with the videos do. When I present this data, I do so with a very strong voice, and I tell a good story. If you haven't read it already, I highly recommend Pat Friman's (2014) paper on public speaking called "Behavior Analysts to the Front! A 15-Step Tutorial on Public Speaking." Friman discusses the importance of being an excellent public speaker while sharing practical tips on how to become one.

List three opportunities you can obtain to support the development of your public speaking skills. Some examples include presenting to your supervisees, submitting a request to present at a conference, or presenting a journal article to your company.

_____

_____

_____

Strategy 11: Network

Although it may not always feel like it, our field is relatively small compared to others. Though growing, it is still of a size where networking with even the top names in our field is possible and can be beneficial. Networking can impact your career as a researcher in several ways. It gets your ideas out there, potentially to key people who may be able to promote you and your research to others, give you new ideas, tell you about related research happening in their labs, and generally be a resource for you. I will never forget the first time at a conference when an invited speaker, a well-known behavior analyst, mentioned my name in his talk. He and I had spoken earlier about a study I was hoping to conduct, and he had given me some valuable insight and recommendations for the experimental design. After that talk, several people approached me to ask about the research, some of whom also gave me additional great ideas.

Conferencing is a great way to network, and there is no shortage of conferences in our field! Becerra et al. (2020) wrote an excellent article discussing the benefits of the conference experience, one of which is networking and socializing. These authors also discuss how to maximize the experience and provide a table that lists all international, national, and regional conferences, along with the month in which they typically occur. I would encourage you to check out their article and map out a plan for conferencing. I typically choose one main conference to attend and attend any others if I am an invited speaker. This typically results in attendance at three to five conferences per year, providing plenty of time for networking. I recommend attending one conference per year, selecting the one that contains content most relevant to your research agenda. Managing expenses can be an important consideration, but if you are presenting on behalf of your organization, your employer may be willing to pay for your conference, or at least part of it, utilizing professional development funds.

Take a moment to think about and list three ways you can network in the next six months. Examples include attending a conference and introducing yourself to someone or emailing someone you know and asking them to introduce you to someone else.

_____

_____

_____

Strategy 12: Become a Good Storyteller

A fantastic piece of advice I was given early in my career as a researcher was that data do not always speak for themselves—so, you must speak for them. Often, data are only as good as the story you tell. While scientific research is often thought of as being overly technical and dry, it does not have to be. Think of the last research article you read that was impactful. What made it so? What did you remember about it? My guess is that the data were interesting, but really what you remember is the story behind the data—the way the author walked you through an applied problem, provided a rationale for asking that certain question, wrote the procedures, and interpreted the results. The discussion section of a manuscript is often where authors get to be a bit more creative—drawing lines and conclusions to get the readers to connect with the data more fully and think, *What next?* Becoming a good storyteller is a practical strategy that will take some time and practice but is important to master. The way to master it is to simply write. Your first few articles are unlikely to have this appeal, but as you get more proficient and start to look at data in new and meaningful ways, your writing will evolve. Try to read articles by authors who are good at this—call out the things that make the article interesting and those that make it boring! Imitation can be powerful— imitate the tone and feel of others' work (as appropriate) to develop your own style that helps you tell a good story.

What is the last research article you read that had an impact on you? Why was it so impactful? List specific things the writer did that made an impression on you and helped tell a good story.

_____

_____

_____

_____

_____

Strategy 13: Build in Downtime to Your Research Schedule

You might be surprised to read this recommendation, particularly if you are breaking research tasks into small chunks and spreading those tasks over several days. However, just like anything you enjoy, if you do too much of it, you will burn out. I commonly write Monday through Friday and take the weekends off. When I return to my task on Monday morning, I feel refreshed and typically stay productive throughout the week. You can choose whatever schedule you like—maybe the weekends are optimal for you, so you decide to take Wednesdays and Thursdays off. Whatever schedule you choose, the key to staying productive when you have breaks in between research time is to take good notes on where you left off. And, if you have a good idea during one of your "off" days, go ahead and write it down so you remember it when you return! Some of my best ideas have come during that downtime when I am not requiring myself to focus on research!

Take a few moments to consider the time during the week you plan to take off from research. This should jibe with the schedule you developed in chapter 5. Jot down a possible research schedule.

_____

_____

_____

_____

Strategy 14: Make Research Social

When Kelley et al. (2015) interviewed prolific practitioner-researchers, two of the behaviors the respondents attributed to their success revolved around being social. Specifically, they recommended that aspiring researchers arrange as much face-to-face time with peer researchers, collaborators, and research supervisees as possible and write the results of research collaboratively. Although physically being in the same room may not be possible due to geography, technology allows us to have web meetings and connect with individuals more easily than ever before. Having regular check-ins with others can not only give you deadlines and accountability, but also make research fun. Having social interaction with others can facilitate creativity and brainstorming—making your ideas and writing better. Everyone falls along a spectrum of how much social behavior they desire in their research endeavors, so you can pick the amount that works best for you and your research team. The amount and type may vary by project too—for example, a literature review paper may be less conducive to collaborative meetings (during the beginning stages especially) than a paper with active data collection to be reviewed, analyzed, and interpreted. Here are some things to do to make your research endeavors social:

1. Arrange for a group of fellow behavior analyst friends to meet at a coffee shop once a month to discuss research and new ideas.

2. Organize a research club at your organization.

3. Schedule regular writing and read-through sessions with coauthors on your papers.

4. Get together with like-minded researchers at conferences and conventions.

5. Schedule regular check-ins with your mentor to review progress, discuss new ideas, and work on your professional development.

Strategy 15: Review Your Accomplishments Regularly

This strategy involves tracking and recording your writing tasks, presentations, and publications. When I began organizing my time, creating task analyses, and strategically planning my research time, I also started a "completed writing" Word document. When I finish a task, I strike through that task on my "writing to-do list" Word document and move it to my separate "completed writing" Word document. My only reason for doing this was that something about deleting the written task altogether made me feel uneasy. I suppose I wanted a record of accomplishments, though I had no intention of doing anything with that list. I started that Word document on August 30, 2017. Today is March 14, 2020, and it is sixteen pages long with over 600 completed tasks! Here is a sample of my completed writing list after I've moved completed tasks over to it:

- **Mand prerequisite revisions**—submit in October
    - ~~Review AE Letter—focus on why need prompt data~~
    - ~~Read old to-do list in notes, determine if still relevant~~
    - ~~Reread original paper~~
    - ~~Decide whether to include prompt data~~
    - ~~Continue AE letter to-do list making comments as you go, make all changes—3 left~~
    - ~~Graphs-should we include them all in the paper?~~
    - ~~Overall review of changes & edit~~
    - ~~Send revised version to coauthors with summary of changes~~
- **JABA review #102**–due 9/29
    - ~~Download article~~

- ~~Print article~~
- ~~Another review of manuscript~~
- ~~Write review in paragraph form~~
- ~~Final review/edit & submit~~

- **JABA review #104**–due 10/5
  - ~~Download article~~
  - ~~Print article~~
  - ~~Read & write bullets~~
  - ~~Review again, write final version in paragraph form~~
  - ~~Go back through JABA review and ensure all bullet points make sense~~
  - ~~Submit through portal!~~

- **Public Speaking Research**—due 10/13
  - ~~Read minutes from meeting on 9/13~~
  - ~~Read public speaking article and come up with some recommendations, identify anything missing, and bring back to research group~~
  - ~~Look through box folder and read other materials/resources—make notes~~

- **COABA Talk**—
  - ~~Read two articles on public speaking~~
  - ~~Find an analogy for disconnect between research and practice~~
  - ~~Research medical support for dietary changes for asthma (if this will be your opener)~~
  - ~~Write sections on Pace~~
  - ~~Write section on sup practice and IV count~~
  - ~~Write framework section & ending~~
  - ~~Time all—see if you want to add extinction induced~~
  - ~~Really time the whole thing perfectly~~
  - ~~Make any final revisions Thurs~~
  - ~~Finish slides for remaining parts of presentation~~
  - ~~Practice with powerpoint and memorize!!~~
  - ~~1-2 more Practice COABA talk in entirety—timed~~

I maintain this document and find that I look at it regularly. It helps motivate me. I see how much I accomplish in a day, week, month, and year and remember that although it sometimes feels like slow progress, the work is paying off.

Another thing I do to track and review my accomplishments is to graph my peer-reviewed publications each year. This visual depiction of publication accomplishments helps me see that those individual writing tasks often result in peer-reviewed publications and also allows me to analyze my yearly contributions to monitor if they increase or decrease. If I have an unusually low or high year, I can look to see what occurred in my life that may have contributed to that change. For example, in 2012 I changed jobs, and, as you can see in the graph below of my publications since 2012, it took a few years for my research to get going again, but it ticked up in 2015.

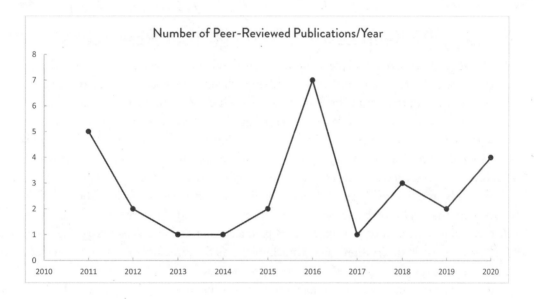

Finally, in addition to tracking your completed writing tasks and your publications, keep your resume or CV up to date. Especially as you present at conferences, the list can get very lengthy and you might begin to forget about certain presentations or even publications. My rule is that as soon as a symposium, panel discussion, or invited speaker talk gets accepted, I add it to my CV. As soon as I receive an "accept" decision on a manuscript, I add it to my CV. You can list work that has been accepted and not published yet ("in press") and work that has been submitted but does not have a decision yet ("under review"), especially in the early phases of your research career when you may not have any publications yet. Including these can encourage you and also tell anyone reviewing your CV that you've been an active researcher, even if nothing is formally published yet.

Take a few moments to describe what documents you will create as permanent products to
review regularly and remind yourself of your accomplishments.

_____

_____

_____

_____

_____

Strategy 16: Keep Learning Through Your Research

As I mentioned in previous chapters, when I began conducting research, I focused primarily
on verbal behavior research with young children with autism. I had a lot to learn and conducting research in this area helped me hone my skills as a practitioner. Of course, I never
got to a point where I felt I had learned everything about verbal behavior, but I did reach a
point in my research career where I became more interested in other areas—specifically
professional practice areas such as ethics and supervision. In 2016, the journal *Behavior
Analysis in Practice* (BAP) made a call for manuscripts for their special issue on supervision.
I had long been interested in supervision from an applied perspective and had been told by
supervisees that I was good at it. So two colleagues and I decided to write several papers for
that special issue, including a recommended practice paper (Sellers, Valentino, & LeBlanc,
2016), one on group supervision (Valentino, LeBlanc, & Sellers, 2016), and another on identifying issues in the supervisory relationship and solving them (Sellers, LeBlanc, & Valentino,
2016). This change in focus helped facilitate more learning and kept me motivated. I felt I
had so much to learn about supervision, and writing helped me learn it. It also opened
several avenues for me. At the time, not much had been published in the area of supervision,
so I quickly made a name for myself in that arena. I began getting invited to speak at conferences on the topic, to sit on award committees reviewing supervisory performance, and to
be a coach for the BACB for the supervision code section. Importantly, I had opportunities
to write more and was asked to write a book chapter on the topic (Valentino, in press)–an
extremely educational experience. By comparison, in my previous research area of verbal
behavior, I had been invited to speak at only one conference and did not have any of the
other experiences. This lack of opportunities existed primarily because there were already
several very good verbal behavior researchers, so there wasn't much room to make that big
of a name in the area. The moral of this story is to keep learning through your research! If
you hit a wall, switch directions and continue to be open to new avenues over the course of
your career.

Strategy 17: Set Bigger Goals

Thus far, I've talked about the importance of establishing big project goals and then breaking those projects down into smaller more manageable goals. Now I want to talk about the opposite—establishing bigger, or *stretch,* goals. This could be something you've always wanted to do (e.g., write a book) or a numerical goal for things you are already doing (e.g., publish three articles a year for the next three years). In 2019, I realized that I had published twenty-two articles in-peer reviewed journals. I had several articles under review, several I was writing, and several I could be writing. In early 2019 I established a fun goal for myself that I called "30 before 20." The goal was simple—to have at least thirty articles accepted for publication or fully published by 2020. It was a bit lofty given the length of time the editorial process can take—but it was doable. I worked hard and am proud to say I made it to... twenty-eight! This big goal helped a ton—when I got discouraged or wanted to cancel writing time, I remembered my goal and how cool it would be to accomplish it. I had it written in a notebook that I carried around and updated often. It was a constant visual reminder of a goal I had set for myself and kept me motivated. You can think about your bigger goals regularly and establish them any time you like—for the year, each quarter, or even every month. I like to have one big goal every year to keep me going. Here are some other examples:

- Get invited to speak at a conference.

- Write a book chapter.

- Present in a symposium at two conferences each year for the next three years.

- Publish one paper per year for the next five years.

- Serve as a reviewer for a peer-reviewed journal.

- Become an associate editor of a journal.

- Review ten articles during the year.

- Start at least one new research project every six months for the next two years.

List your own "big goals" here. Make a plan and timeline to accomplish them!

_____

_____

_____

_____

_____

Strategy 18: Have Accountability to Others

If you are working with other researchers (which you often are), accountability to others comes naturally through that collaboration. Your coauthors will be relying on you to meet deadlines, collect data, write, and even lead the team. In addition to the natural social contingencies provided by your research team, there are other ways to embed accountability into your research.

For many years, the organization where I work had a wonderful postdoctoral fellowship program. The program was designed to give new graduates the opportunity to experience 50% clinical work and 50% research in an applied setting. The setup is ideal, but inevitably the clinical work would often take priority as research was easy to put to the side. One of the most common occurrences I observed is that post docs came into the position with good intentions to write their dissertation up for publication but often got distracted by clinical work or other applied studies. I supervised many of these post docs, and in the second year of doing so I began an accountability procedure for them. I had them set deadlines for their project (usually their dissertation). Then, we created calendar appointments for each of those deadlines. The post doc was required to email me each portion of their manuscript by the deadline. These were not projects I was involved in at all, so I did not read the manuscripts or give any kind of feedback. I was merely setting up accountability and structure that they did not have. It worked very well! I too, have done similar things in my research career. Especially in the beginning, I would often ask my supervisor or a colleague if I could email them something by a certain date. The individual was not involved in my work, but having someone else know that I had a deadline to meet and to be on the lookout for the final product is the exact thing I needed to hold me accountable. It's a lot like telling people you are trying to eat healthily. Just the mere act of doing so increases the likelihood you will make healthy choices (at least around other people, any way!).

List some ways you can embed accountability into your work week, focusing specifically on the people who can help hold you accountable.

_____

_____

_____

_____

_____

_____

_____

_____

Essential Takeaways

This chapter offered several practical strategies for conducting research, from making initial decisions about what you want to research to holding yourself accountable to others. Your life will change over time and you'll need to adapt accordingly, but using these strategies and incorporating them into your life will ensure you can not only start but maintain a research career.

CHAPTER 8

Receiving Mentorship

If you do not have one already, I recommend identifying a mentor—someone who can mentor you specifically in applied research. Ideally this person will also be an applied researcher; however, you could easily receive mentorship from people with a different career profile and still benefit greatly. Much of your experience and development will come from this research mentor—someone who can give you opportunities, teach you new skills, and challenge you to become a very effective and skilled practitioner-researcher. In this chapter, I'll discuss all phases of the mentoring relationship: identifying characteristics of a mentor, finding a research mentor, connecting with your mentor, organizing your time, getting the most out of the relationship, maintaining it, and finally transitioning from it. I will conclude with advice on how to and why you should mentor others when you are ready to do so in your career.

Characteristics of a Mentor

You've likely heard of mentors and probably have one. A mentor is someone you can trust—someone who trains and teaches. While you may have had a mentor in your professional life, now you're looking for a research mentor. This person should have all the qualities you'd commonly look for in a professional mentor: likeability, empathy, warmth, knowledge, and dependability. You'll also want them to have specific experiences—preferably conducting applied research. This could be an existing professional mentor with whom you can continue to deepen your relationship, focusing specifically on research. Otherwise, it is helpful to identify someone whose career path is like yours. There are no hard and fast rules for the specific experiences one must have to be a good mentor. In fact, I think this is highly individualized—a mentor who is a good fit for one person may be a terrible fit for another.

Think about the qualities you want in a mentor and list them here.

_____

_____

_____

_____

How to Find a Research Mentor

For some, this may be the most challenging part of beginning a mentor relationship—finding the right person. First, find someone you like and admire. You might recall impactful talks you have attended at professional conferences or journal articles you've read. At this stage, don't worry if you think the person will say no. Simply start a list of people you like and admire. Remember, you only need to find one mentor! After you've made your list, read up on each person a little more. Where are they located in the country? What are their current interests? Have you read their latest research? Do you know anybody who knows them?

Think about your goals and what you want to accomplish with your mentor. Have clear expectations for what this person can help you with before approaching them—this will make narrowing down that initial list easier and will make the conversation about mentoring clearer. You might consider talking to other people who have mentors (specifically, research mentors) and finding out what they like about that person, how the dynamic works, and why. Finally, consider personality traits—if someone you admire conducts research but is known for treating people poorly or exhibiting other undesirable personality traits, they may not offer you much in the way of support—even if they are very knowledgeable.

Here is a sample list of people (the names are fictional, but this will give you an idea of how you might construct a similar list based on actual behavior analysts).

1. **George Cast**—he presented a cool study on verbal behavior a few years ago at the ABAI annual convention in San Diego. He had captured some interesting skills that are needed to teach specific repertoires and it was something I had been struggling with clinically for a while.

2. **Ebony Street**—I met her once at a local conference and we chatted about her research on supervision. It was in its beginning stages, but I remember really liking her approach and how easy she was to talk with.

3. **Garth Smith**—He is a pioneer in the ethics world and has published a book and several hallmark articles on ethics. I am very interested in ethics but need a lot of support, as it's a new area for me to venture into, especially in the research world.

4. **Grey Stone**—Grey and I have known each other for a long time. He works at an agency that is of similar size and structure to mine. He published unique work on the assessment and treatment of problem behavior. I think I could learn a lot from him.

5. **Olivia Torres**—She publishes in the organizational behavior management literature a lot. She does staff training work that would be super applicable to my company. I think she found a way to conduct research and consult with companies about their training procedures, which means she'd likely be able to mentor me in having a discussion with my organization about starting research activity.

Finally, our field offers some opportunities for mentorship through different programs. For example, the group Women in Behavior Analysis offers the opportunity for women to mentor others. You can contact them via their website (https://www.thebaca.com/about-wiba/) for details. Later in your research career, if you conduct reviews for journals and become skilled in this area, some journals, such as the *Journal of Applied Behavior Analysis,* have formal associate editor mentoring programs. These programs typically last one year and involve setting you up with a past or present associate editor who teaches you about how to serve as an associate editor. These are very special and unique positions and ones you need to be invited to participate in, but they do exist for individuals who have contributed to the literature over a long period of time and have the right skills to serve the journal well.

How to Connect with a Mentor

First and foremost, you should be prepared for some people to be uninterested in mentoring. However, there are actions you can take to increase the likelihood that someone will be interested. If you already have an individual in your world who could serve as a research mentor, you may not even have to formally ask them to be your mentor, which can be awkward. In fact, most mentoring relationships start with a mutual connection and evolve over time. If you already work and collaborate with that person in some capacity, you could simply start steering the conversations and questions to applied research. It may be helpful to mention to them that you have professional interests to conduct more research and think that you have a lot to learn from them. Most people will not cut off the relationship simply because you want to discuss other topics. You might consider the frequency of your interactions and whether that frequency needs to change. If it does, make that known to your mentor so they can determine a workable schedule.

It's likely that you do not have someone you are already connected with, in which case you will need to establish the relationship from scratch. I do not recommend directly asking someone to be your mentor. It is likely to catch them off guard, and without full context or knowing you very well, they are likely to review their time commitments and conclude they do not have time and do not have much to get out of the relationship. Instead, you should start small by sending them an email or introducing yourself at a conference. Mention that you like their work or are following their latest research projects. You could also simply comment on something you appreciate about them—their presentation style, friendly interactions with others, professional presence, and so on.

Once you've had a few interactions, you can assess whether you might be a good match with the individual and if you are, decide whether you can begin to establish the relationship, for example, by volunteering to do some work for them in exchange for learning. Volunteering to help them out in some way is an excellent strategy and may result in your never having to formally ask the question.

This is exactly how my relationship with my research mentor came about. I was new to an organization and did not have much exposure to the person I wanted to be my mentor. She was several positions above me and while she knew me, we didn't have any time carved out specifically to touch base. There was also already a research director. When that research director went out on maternity leave, I asked if I could volunteer to help with some of her tasks—lead research meetings, put presentations together, update our literature search request spreadsheet, and manage some of the requests. Of course, my mentor said yes! I worked very hard on those tasks (in addition to my regular clinical position with no changes to it) and the mentoring relationship evolved very naturally, continuing on for several years. Most people will accept your offer to help, and this creates a situation where they get something out of mentoring you, which makes the ask more reasonable.

List five possible research mentors and their contact information here. Make a few notes about their areas of expertise and comment on why you've chosen them as an ideal mentor. List them in order of preference.

1. **Research mentor 1:** Name _____, contact information

    _____, reasons for choosing

    _____

2. **Research mentor 2:** Name _____, contact information

    _____, reasons for choosing

    _____

3. **Research mentor 3:** Name _____, contact information

    _____, reasons for choosing

    _____

4. **Research mentor 4:** Name _____, contact information

    _____, reasons for choosing

    _____

5. **Research mentor 5:** Name _____, contact information

    _____, reasons for choosing

    _____

Here are some talking points you can use to connect with a potential mentor, via either phone or email:

1. State your interest in their work.

2. Acknowledge that you have valued the time you have spent with them thus far.

3. Identify what you have learned from working with them.

4. Express your desire to continue learning about research.

5. Identify what you may be able to help them with (e.g., data collection, graphing).

6. Propose that you continue meeting on a regular basis to obtain research support and help them with the tasks you've identified (e.g., data collection, graphing).

How to Organize the Mentoring Relationship

Now that you've established a mentoring relationship, be thoughtful about how and when you meet with your mentor. It is likely that your interactions are extra and not part of your or their typical work life; thus, you should be considerate of your mentor's time and protective of yours. Your mentor has committed time and energy to you, so be sure to respect that. Be prepared to ask questions and provide regular updates. Your mentor will want to know about your progress regularly. Ask questions that only your mentor can answer and avoid engaging in excessive small talk—focus on career goals, obtaining new knowledge, and exploring research interests. Be prepared for your mentor to give you direct feedback and if you are not getting it, ask for it. For example, ask, "What can I do better? How can I improve? What deficits do you notice in my research repertoire and what should I do to teach myself new skills?"

Here are some topics you can discuss during your time with your mentor:

- A recent article you read

- An idea you have for a research project

- A talk you attended at a conference

- Time management

- Fitting research into clinical work

- Obstacles you are encountering with data collection

- Research ethics

- Ideal participants for a study

- How your mentor utilizes resources to accomplish tasks

- Verbal behavior concepts

- Conceptualization of responding in a research study

- How to network with others at an upcoming conference

- Data-based decision making

- Advanced experimental design

- Appropriate journal outlets for your work

- The editorial process and what to expect upon submission

- Writing a cover letter for a manuscript submission

- Respectfully following up with the editor of a journal about the status of your work

Additionally, here are things you can do with your mentor:

- Share data and review it

- Interpret data

- Review your manuscript writing and get feedback

- Review a presentation you are going to give

- Problem solve when a study does not go as planned

I recommend hashing out a schedule in advance that includes face-to-face or remote meetings, email conversations, and phone calls. It will be beneficial to get into a rhythm. There are no hard and fast rules here, so you can meet as frequently or infrequently as needed. The way in which you stay connected can vary too. Here is a sample schedule:

Meet every other Tuesday at 9 a.m. for one hour for discussion, planning, and support.

Stay connected via email as needed.

Plan to meet in person twice per year at conferences you both will attend.

How to Get the Most out of Time with Your Mentor

Now that you've identified the characteristics you are looking for in a mentor, have found your mentor, and have organized your time, you might be wondering how to get the most out of your time with that person. You might be overwhelmed with things to talk about or feel like you are not sure where to start. You can structure your time in the way that feels most consistent with your needs—there are no rules here. The important thing is to value and respect the time you have together. If you are struggling to get started or make the most out of your time, here are some more detailed topics/discussion starters to support you in getting information and to facilitate your learning:

1. Ask your mentor how they became interested in applied research. Was it an intentional career path and plan? How did they carve out opportunities to explore this interest?

2. Explore how and why you became interested in research. Reflecting out loud with your mentor may help you identify motivation and important goals for the future.

3. Ask your mentor what their three main barriers were to conducting research in an applied setting and how they overcame those barriers.

4. Discuss how to appeal to leadership of a for-profit company—what are the selling points that made research appealing to your mentor's organization and what was their role in starting the research culture, if there is one?

5. Present your research schedule and task lists to your mentor and ask them to critique them. Are you spending too much time on one task, not allotting enough time to any of them?

6. Ask your mentor who their mentor was and what they've learned from that person.

7. Discuss the importance of public speaking and ask your mentor to give you tips. When you have a presentation coming up, ask to practice it in front of them and get feedback.

8. Inquire about research mistakes your mentor has made and what they learned from them.

9. Have your mentor share things they wish they would have known early in their research career.

10. Ask your mentor to share their research schedule, to-do list, and tasks. How do they prioritize their time? When do they shift focus?

11. Find out if there has ever been a time when your mentor stopped researching. What caused them to do so? Why did they pick back up again?

12. What is your mentor's teaching philosophy? How do they conceptualize teaching others about research? What have they found to be successful? What have they found to be unsuccessful in their training efforts?

13. Discuss work-life balance. Since both of you likely fit research into your world even though it isn't a formal part of your job, how does your research mentor foster their research interests while maintaining their other job responsibilities and a social/ family life?

14. If your mentor runs into a researcher they admire at a conference, how do they approach that person (if they do at all)? Do they have tips for networking and getting the most out of these encounters?

15. What is a skill your mentor is still working on and trying to develop? This could facilitate a discussion on lifelong learning, how priorities shift over time, and what becomes important in an applied researcher's later career.

16. What is your mentor's favorite research study they have ever published? Why? How can you take what they share with you and consider your own research interests and motivation for your work?

17. Ask your mentor to tell you about an ethical dilemma they faced when conducting research. How did they manage it and what did they learn? How did they adapt their research practices to prevent it from happening again?

18. Where does your research mentor see themself in five years? Ten years? This discussion could help you conceptualize your own long-term research goals.

19. How does your research mentor define success in their research endeavors? What do they look for in terms of their own accomplishments and feedback from others to determine their success? Consider their responses in the context of your own goals for your research career.

20. How will your mentor know they've been successful in mentoring you? What are the things they will look for to feel productive and successful in the relationship?

21. Ask your mentor about their dissertation or master's thesis. Many individuals stop talking about their original work later in their career, but a lot can be learned from their experience. What did they study and why? Did the study ever get published?

How to Maintain the Relationship

The most important thing is to stay connected with your mentor, especially if you are not often physically in the same place. It can be easy to cancel or reschedule a meeting when life gets hectic, which is likely to quickly result in the relationship's dissolving. Show up to meetings, respond to emails, and complete volunteer work. Check in often to ensure you are both getting something out of the work you are doing together. There will be a time when you're not, but if you are, you should continue meeting. Assess whether you need to change anything about your connections—the time, place, frequency, or duration—and change it.

Sellers, LeBlanc, and Valentino (2016) provide guidance to supervisors to identify and address barriers to a supervisory relationship. This guidance is focused on supervisor/supervisee relationships that exist for supporting a supervisee in becoming a BCBA. However, many of the ideas can be applied to the mentoring relationship. The three main barriers these authors address are (1) disorganization and poor time management, (2) poor interpersonal skills, and (3) difficulty accepting and applying feedback. Although these may not pop up as often in a mentor/mentee relationship, checking in on any issues that may arise using this framework can be helpful. If both parties remain committed to the mentoring relationship, problem solving early on can help it thrive.

Note: This activity may be best to complete after you've arranged and begun a mentoring relationship with someone.

List five active ways you can maintain your mentoring relationship. Examples include the following: commit to a schedule, show up for meetings, send an agenda ahead of time, praise your mentor for their support and teaching, assess time commitment and adapt as needed, be flexible, commit to learning new things, commit to open communication and feedback.

_____

_____

_____

_____

_____

_____

_____

How and When to Transition out of the Relationship

Mentoring relationships can last a variable amount of time—from a few months, to several years, to the course of one's entire career. There are no hard and fast rules about the length of time you should be mentored or mentor someone. The decision to transition out of the mentoring relationship may occur gradually over time, and often is made quite naturally. For example, one individual may change jobs, making them physically farther away or less available. Perhaps schedules will change, and meetings will become less frequent.

If you are being mentored, the important question to ask yourself is *Do I continue to learn and grow as a result of my interactions with this individual?* Ask yourself whether the frequency, duration, and nature of your interactions are still beneficial and worth your time. It is possible that you still benefit from interacting with the individual but could do so less often or in a different way. I do not believe anyone ever formally stops being your mentor—I think the relationship evolves over time and the actual time spent together may lessen or change.

In my own professional life, I had one mentoring relationship that simply stopped because I changed jobs. Another one just slowly changed as we both switched positions. Eventually, one of my mentors left the organization where I was still employed and I became more confident and competent in my research abilities. I still reach out to some of my mentors and try to get together with them at annual conferences or events. However, I do not spend time formally meeting with them regularly, observing their work, or asking questions.

I recommend continuing the mentoring relationship for as long as it is beneficial for you both and then letting it end or change naturally as mine have. If it does not and there is a need to make a change (e.g., you are having issues that cannot be overcome), a more formal ending to the relationship may need to occur—this is likely best done through a professional conversation and agreement to stop meeting. It is highly likely you both are aware of any issues that exist, so approaching the conversation should be easy and you can come to an agreement about the change.

Identify three ways you will know it is time to transition out of the formal mentoring relationship. Examples include a life change, decrease in topics to discuss, natural change of schedules, increase in other commitments that make it difficult to adhere to your schedule and commitments, your desire to transition to researching a new topic/work with a new mentor, personality conflicts, and repetition of topics or conversations.

How to Mentor Someone Else

Thus far, we have spoken about finding a mentor and being a mentee. There will be a time in your career where you become the mentor. Being a mentor is an extremely important role for our field. It is the primary way through which we support, train, and invest in the next generation of behavior analysts. Mentors provide their mentees with personal growth and professional socialization. Research mentors teach critical new skills that will support high-quality practical research for the future. Just as with formal supervision or graduate school advisement, the more people you supervise over the course of your career, the more people you will impact. You're impacting not only your mentees, but the people they mentor, the people their mentees mentor and so on. Additionally, their clients, coworkers, and the field will be influenced by your mentorship. If you have never been a mentor before, that is okay! You've spent the last several years (likely) being mentored, so you have at least one model to imitate, and you can start there. Imitate the characteristics and behaviors you enjoyed about your mentor. Consider things you'd do differently. While you might start off doing things exactly like your mentor, over time you should work on developing your own style. Your interactions with your mentee and others will shape your behavior and the mentor you will become. It is an exciting process to take part in, and, particularly if you are mentoring someone specifically about research, it means you have accomplished much of what you set out to do! While you are likely not done growing as a researcher, this hallmark time means you have accomplished enough to teach someone else how to do the same. So, if someone asks you the big question, "Will you be my mentor?"—say YES!

Take a few moments to identify the things you have to offer as a mentor. Examples include teaching about time management, clinical expertise, desire to learn about _____ area of behavior analysis together, time to give, motivation, and excitement.

_____

_____

_____

_____

_____

Essential Takeaways

Consider a research mentor as a critical resource for you as an applied researcher. Start by considering whether you already have someone in your life who could fulfill this role and if you do not, identify the characteristics of a person you'd like to begin working with. Then follow the steps outlined in this chapter to identify, communicate with, and maintain a relationship with a mentor, all of which will likely happen over a long period of time. When the relationship is no longer beneficial or feasible for one or both of you, transition out of the formal relationship, while hopefully maintaining a lasting connection of some sort. Later in your career you will likely have the privilege of mentoring others who are newer to the field.

CHAPTER 9

Tips for Writing

For many people, writing can seem overwhelming. I've spoken to many behavior analysts wishing to conduct research who feel that they cannot be researchers because of the need to write. It is not uncommon for me to hear things like "I'm just not a good writer." This often occurs because they received negative feedback from a professor or didn't do well in certain classes in college and this idea just stuck. If you feel this way, there is good news! Just like any other behavior, writing is a behavior that can be learned, shaped, and improved over time. You can't improve something you don't do—so the first step is to simply start writing. In this chapter, I'll provide several tips for making the writing process less intimidating and some things you can do in the short term to improve your writing.

Tip #1: Don't overthink it. Too many people spend time overthinking their writing—trying to get the perfect sentence, writing and rewriting it repeatedly, researching synonyms of words to use to improve their written vocabulary, and so on. This is a never-ending trap and one that will keep you from getting good ideas on paper. When you begin writing, do just that—write! Don't overthink it; get your ideas on paper. Do not worry about grammar, vocabulary, or even complete sentences. You might find that your initial draft is actually pretty good. Anything that needs to be polished can be polished later if you have the core ideas and thoughts written down—so start there!

Tip #2: Decide whether or not to outline. Most people will tell you to write an outline. I have a secret—I never make a formal outline. I've tried to use one and it just does not work for me. Now, that's not to say I don't think through and generally jot down some notes about what I want to say. I just don't do a formal outline like my high school English teacher would have suggested I do. This is a highly personal decision and you should try both—try writing with an outline and try writing without one. What feels most natural? What works for you? Do you spend more time writing the outline than writing the paper? The important lesson here is that you should feel free to question conventional wisdom on this type of thing and do what works best for you.

Tip #3: Learn and use APA style. If you do not have a copy of the most recent *Publication Manual of the American Psychological Association* (7th edition; American Psychological Association [APA], 2020), purchase it and begin reviewing it. This will be a great investment and will save you and your AE a ton of time. If your paper is full of editorial problems and stylistic errors, the AE may not be able to see past them, and even if your paper is good, they may provide a not-so-favorable review due to these errors. Writing is much easier when you know most of the rules. Keep it on your desk (or desktop, if you're using the digital version) while writing so you can look up what you don't know. Of course, you do not need to memorize the manual, but having the basics down will help your writing flow and save you editing time on the back end. The APA Style website (https://apastyle.apa.org) also has lots of great resources, including tutorials for learning the guidelines and what's new in the 7th edition.

Tip #4: Let the editorial process work for you. Your paper will not be perfect when you submit it, and that is okay. You should do your part to edit your work and submit a paper that has as few errors as possible, but in the end, you won't catch everything. This is exactly what the editorial process is for and the reason that there are multiple layers of support—the reviewers, associate editor, and editor. They will be reviewing your paper with fresh eyes and will catch many things you won't. So do not sit on a paper revising it time and time again before submission. Review, edit, and submit so you can get the support from the experts in polishing it and getting it ready for publication.

Tip # 5: Make your writing approachable. Even with technical writing, people want to be able to easily digest your words. If you spend a lot of time writing in a way that is overly structured and formal, you may miss your audience. Depending on the journal and type of article, you can take some liberties with decreasing formality and writing like you would typically speak. On this note, you should also review sample journal articles that are like yours—ones that you personally enjoy reading. Get a feel for the author's tone and style and try to mimic it, at least until you develop your own style. Ask for feedback, especially early on in your career. Perhaps a trusted friend, colleague, or mentor would be willing to review your paper and give you feedback—not necessarily on the logistics, but just generally on how the paper reads. Is it easy to understand? Does it flow well? Is it overly wordy with excess detail? Not enough detail? Does it have the intended impact you want it to have? These early reviews from people you trust can help you develop your style in the long term and provide valuable feedback on how readers will feel reviewing your work.

Tip # 6: Always properly cite your work. If you are not sure whether something needs to be cited or not, err on the safe side and cite it (if you are asking whether it does or not, it's highly likely it does anyway!). In this area, your knowledge of the APA style guide will come in handy—there are several guidelines associated with how to cite different types of work, and you will want to follow those guidelines throughout your manuscript and in your final reference section. Remember that even if you were the author on a paper you wish to cite, you need to cite that work the same way you would anybody else's.

Tip #7: Do a final read through, but don't overdo it. You should do a final read through of your paper, but not multiple read throughs. This advice follows along the lines of test taking—it generally is not a good idea to keep going back and changing your answers unless you have very good reason to believe your first response was incorrect. Going with your initial gut reaction will likely prove more valuable, and the same goes for writing. If you decided to describe something a certain way, and you've read through your description once and it makes sense, you are likely best off leaving it as is. Some researchers choose to do read-aloud reviews where they meet with their coauthors and read the paper through together. Individuals can make comments on how the various sections sound and often can directly edit the paper according to the group's consensus. This can be a useful exercise, particularly for papers that may be highly technical or conceptual in nature. If you choose to do the final read through alone, it is useful to do so out loud in some regard—perhaps whispering to yourself. This can help you understand how the sentences sound when read fully through, which may be different than a silent review on your own. I also recommend reviewing in chunks instead of one full read through, particularly if you are reviewing it alone. Your brain can fatigue easily, and you may skip through the later sections or miss errors altogether. Make it a goal to review one section at a time, perhaps over the course of a day or a few days, making changes as you go along. If needed for flow, you can always go back and read the end part of a previous section to refresh your memory before reviewing the next one. Commit to your final review, schedule it, make those changes, and submit your paper!

Tip #8: Match your manuscript to the article type. This seems obvious, but it can be common for authors to review the specific journal but not the paper category and thus have a mismatch between their work and their chosen manuscript type. As an example, *Behavior Analysis in Practice* has a "brief practice" category. This category is meant to facilitate modern practices by reaching the practitioner community quickly. Within this manuscript category, there are several requirements, including a summary of the take-home points for practitioners and a detailed methods section by which people can replicate the procedures in practice. If you decide to submit a manuscript under this category, you'll want to be sure your paper meets these requirements, based on both the big-picture purpose of it and the specifications that must be present in the manuscript.

Tip# 9: Take writing breaks. Writing a technical manuscript is difficult work, and if you take on too much at once, you are bound to burn out. Even if you successfully submit one manuscript, you may feel too exhausted to tackle the next. So take breaks, especially during the writing phase. The amount of time and type of breaks is completely up to you, but having a break in screen time and focused writing time can help improve creativity and focus.

Tip #10: Write what you enjoy writing. You will likely try writing different types of papers over the course of your career and find what you are passionate about. For example, some people love the details involved in writing literature review papers and others love the novelty of discussion papers focused on new practice guidelines. Or, you might geek out over data-based studies and enjoy focusing your time on data interpretation and analysis. Whatever you find you enjoy the most, do a lot of it! You will probably always engage in all types of writing, but when you find your passion, try to focus the bulk of your work on that. This will keep you motivated and avoid writer's burnout over time.

Tip #11: Tell a story. Even though your research writing will be technical in nature, that does not mean you can't be creative and tell a story. Indeed, your data are only as good as the story you tell about them. Think through your procedures, how they came about, and how the participants responded and provide interesting context for your findings. This will keep readers engaged and stimulated by your work.

Tip #12: Control your writing environment. Where you write is just as important as what you write. Being in an environment that stimulates creativity and motivates you is important for your overall research productivity. In chapter 7, I encouraged you to think through the environmental variables that make you feel relaxed and focused. These environmental variables will be important to stick with, especially during your heavy writing times. Also note that they may change over time. For example, you might begin by enjoying music in the background but find that over time it gets very distracting and you need to remove it in order to focus on your writing. Use the Research Environment Worksheet in chapter 7 (also available on the book's website, http://www.newharbinger.com/47827) regularly to determine the best environmental arrangement for you and change it as needed.

Tip #13: Stay positive. It can be very discouraging to receive rejection decisions or critical reviews from journal reviewers and AEs. Some reviewers can be less than kind, and you might be tempted to throw in the towel, especially if you get several reviews that criticize your work. Try to remain positive and know that this is exactly what the review process is for—to provide you with critical feedback that you can use to improve. Do not take it personally. Also know that if a reviewer is very negative, it's likely the review is less about you and more about them. Reviewers are encouraged to have a positive tone, so if this does not occur, it is not usually in line with the journal's mission and is an atypical experience. I highly recommend going through the AE letter and reviews and highlighting the positive parts of your work. Read those first and focus on what you did well, incorporating the areas for improvement after.

Tip #14: Incorporate feedback. You will become a better researcher and writer if you incorporate others' feedback into your work. Avoid the temptation to get defensive and keep doing things the same way you have always done them. While you might not follow every piece of advice from your mentor, peers, or the review panel, take each one and consider how it might make your work better, incorporating those you find most valuable.

Tip #15: Occasionally, write on your own. Meaning, be the sole author of a paper from time to time. Collaborating is amazing, and often you will have coauthors on your work due to the collaborative nature of our field. However, it can be very useful to be the only author on a paper. Set a goal for yourself to write one paper where you are the sole author. Doing so will force you to write the way you want to write and to get feedback on your work through the editorial process. When you collaborate on a paper, the feedback you receive applies to the work the group put forth. But when you author a paper on your own, you are putting forward your ideas and your writing only. Thus, the feedback given will be valuable as you go along your research journey. While it may not be possible to be the sole author frequently (it's a lot of work!), after your initial sole-author paper, assess the experience and how much value it added to your writing experience. If it was indeed positive and valuable, set a goal to author a paper once every few years, or more frequently if it is possible for you to do so. Very early in my career, I attempted to author a paper on my own. It was a brief review. The editor rejected it without even sending it out to a review panel. It was a good exercise for me, but I wasn't quite ready to solely author a paper yet. Years later, I was able to successfully do so, but I had a lot more systems in place to support this goal. My writing was also much better!

Tip #16: Write outside the field. It can be immensely helpful (if one of your projects is fitting) to publish in a journal outside of behavior analysis. This will require you to reduce technical jargon and explain procedures in a way that will appeal to individuals who may not have vast knowledge of the ABA literature base from which your work was drawn. Consider related fields like special education, psychology, or counseling and choose one of your pieces of work to target this different audience. Not only will you be helping our science stretch to other fields, but you'll be practicing a different set of writing skills.

Tip # 17: Write other things. By "things," I mean blogs, entries for newsletters, and even personal journal entries. Doing so will decrease the stress you may feel with always doing technical writing and will give you the ability to express yourself in a different way. The more you write, the better you will get at it, and learning how to adapt your style to different mediums and audiences will support versatility in your writing, improving it overall.

Essential Takeaways

Many people think they are not great writers for one reason or another. I encourage you to dismiss this idea and begin to home in on the skills you need to develop and the ones you already have. By using the tips in this chapter, you can improve your writing. You'll also develop your own writing style, which is more important than getting your writing "right." Every writer starts somewhere, and this is your starting point!

CHAPTER 10

A Guide to the Editorial Process

We've covered everything you need to know about conducting research and writing—except how to steer through the editorial process. Navigating different scientific journals can be challenging at the start of your publishing career. Thus, it will be helpful to know basic information about the journal so you can approach the process confidently. In this chapter, I outline general information about journals for you to be aware of, such as what an impact factor is, the different roles people play when reviewing your manuscript, and the most common types of article submission categories. Then, I dive into the specifics of how to submit a manuscript and what to expect before, during, and after you receive an editorial decision.

Journal Information

You've written your manuscript and are now hoping to get it published in a reputable journal. Where do you begin? What do you need to consider? There are a variety of journals to choose from and you may not know which one is the right fit for your paper. Below, I describe factors for you to consider to find the perfect outlet for your work.

Impact factor

An impact factor is a scientific metric based on number of citations that is used to gauge the importance of a journal in a field. The impact factor is calculated yearly and takes into consideration the average number of citations that occurred in a year along with the number of articles published in that journal during the preceding two years. The higher the impact factor, the better the journal. A good impact factor varies by field and a very small percentage of journals have an impact factor higher than 10. You can find a journal's impact factor by visiting its website.

It is good to know a journal's impact factor before you decide to submit an article for publication. It can be helpful in allowing you to understand the impact your article may have on the field. As an example, one journal in our field that you are likely very familiar with is the *Journal of Applied Behavior Analysis* (JABA), which I've discussed several times in this book given its relevance to the topic. In 2020, its impact factor was 1.54. You might consider this impact factor number against other factors such as the prestige of the journal, its mission, peer review, readership, and categories of articles you can submit when considering whether it might be a good fit for your work. Consider the decision of which journal to submit your manuscript to as an exercise in finding the right "match"—that is, does your work jibe well with the journal's mission and will publication in that journal help you reach your intended audience?

Take a few moments to choose a journal you might be interested in publishing in. Then, see if you can locate the impact factor. List that information here:

Journal: _____

Impact Factor: _____

Peer Review

A journal may or may not have a peer-review process. Peer review is considered best because it means that the manuscripts published have been reviewed by at least one other peer—commonly more than that—including the editor or an associate editor, and a panel of anywhere from one to five subject matter experts (reviewers). Some journals may have a process wherein the editor reviews the manuscript and acts as the sole peer reviewer, though this is uncommon. Be wary of journals that publish articles as they are, without any form of review; while this may make for an "easy" publication, the quality of the manuscripts published in that journal is likely to be poor and the manuscript may not be cited very often because of this.

Even when a journal is peer reviewed, the quality of the peer-review process can vary significantly by journal and by field. Some peer reviewers simply review the manuscript and make a decision, whereas others scrutinize the manuscript and provide critical feedback (sometimes multiple pages) to support the authors in developing their manuscript more fully. Behavior analytic journals are known for having a very detailed and solid peer-review process. The general mentality across most journals is to provide a critique in a positive tone and to reinforce an individual's contributions, even if the ultimate decision is to reject the manuscript. Behavior analysts take this approach because it is critical to the growth of our field for individuals to begin and continue publishing. Thus, it is important for researchers to have a positive experience and to learn from the publication process so they can make changes to future work and increase the likelihood of publication or simply to improve their research procedures and writing. To find out if the manuscript is peer reviewed, you can look on the journal's website. If the information is not available on the website, you can email the editor directly to ask about the peer-review process.

Take a few moments to choose a journal you might be interested in publishing in. Then, see if you can identify if the journal is peer reviewed or not. List that information here:

Journal: _____

Peer reviewed? _____

Readership

It is extremely important to identify the readership, or target audience, before deciding whether to submit to a journal. There should be a good match between your article's focus and your audience. If you do not have a match, the manuscript could be rejected from the journal immediately, or if it does get accepted it may not be read often because the readership either is uninterested or does not have the appropriate background to benefit from it. For example, if you write an article focused on efficient teaching procedures in a classroom setting and you want that article to be accessed by special education teachers, submitting it to a journal with a primary readership of experimental psychologists would be a poor match. This is an obvious example, and in behavior analysis the distinction can be a bit more subtle. For example, perhaps a researcher in academia writes an article that is translational in nature but submits that article to a journal primarily focused on ABA practitioners. Unless the article contains specific instructions on what can be gathered from the data and how practitioners could use the information, the article will not be well suited for that readership.

Before you begin writing and sometimes even before you begin developing an idea, you should identify your audience. While you do not need to identify the specific journal (though you could), you should know whom your data or discussion is intended to reach. Doing so will help you write toward that audience and may dictate which components of your paper you add versus avoid discussing. I have served as an associate editor for two behavior analytic journals and as a reviewer for over a dozen journals, and this is a very common piece of feedback I provide: "Your study is interesting, but it does not appeal to the readership of this particular journal. A journal focused on ____ is likely to be a better match." *Behavior Analysis in Practice* (BAP) is a popular journal in our field. Its target audience includes frontline service workers and their supervisors, scientist-practitioners, and school personnel. Thus, any papers submitted to BAP should include a focus on this population—findings that can support their practice or enable them to supervise more effectively or implement new evidence-based procedures into their work are most valuable.

Take a few moments to choose a journal you might be interested in publishing in. Then, see if you can locate the target audience. List that information here:

Journal: _____

Target Audience: _____

The Journal's Mission

Every journal also has a mission, and that mission is equally important to its target audience, impact factor, and general readership. You want to choose a journal whose mission matches your research study. This can be a bit more difficult to do, as mission statements are sometimes vague. However, when paired with knowledge about the target audience and impact of the journal, you can identify whether your paper will make a good match for that journal. This mission statement can sometimes be labeled "aim" or "aims and scope." As an example, BAP's mission is to "promote empirically validated best practices in an accessible format that describes not only what works, but also the challenges of implementation in practical settings." Given this information, you would choose this journal if your manuscript addresses a practical issue that would be easily digested by a practitioner population.

Take a few moments to choose a journal you might be interested in publishing in. Then, see if you can locate the journal's mission. List that information here:

Journal: _____

Mission: _____

Types of Manuscripts

Each journal will have a unique set of article types it accepts, which match the journal's mission and target audience. Prior to choosing a journal and writing, review the types of articles and ensure your work will fit within that category. Here are some common examples of article types you will find in behavior analytic journals. Note that the description will vary a bit depending on the journal, so use these descriptions to get a broad understanding of the category and then review the journal's specific requirements once you've decided on a journal.

Research article. These are data-based studies that use single-case design or group design. The content should focus on the journal's mission—for example, a research article published in the journal *The Analysis of Verbal Behavior* (TAVB) should have verbal behavior as the topic. Research articles typically pertain to studies with multiple participants, though very innovative work with a small number of participants that demonstrates strong experimental control could be published as a research article. Manuscripts of this type should be empirical, containing direct behavioral measures—meaning papers without direct behavioral data would fall into a different type of manuscript.

Technical/tutorial article. These manuscripts are used for descriptions of policies or procedures that may be complex but are relevant to the journal's target audience. You might see manuscripts on topics such as electronic data collection, legal issues regarding licensure, medical issues facing a certain population, or graphing. Typically, authors of technical articles have expertise on the topic of interest, leaving them well suited to educate the field accordingly.

Brief report. Brief reports are typically data based and may include pilot studies. It is more common to see a brief report with only one participant, though more than one can be included, and the same rigor on experimental control applies here as it does in research articles. There are typically word limits associated with a brief report, such that they are concise and easy to quickly digest.

Brief practice. This category is specific to a popular journal in our field, *Behavior Analysis in Practice* (BAP), and focuses on application of our science within a practice context. There are specific guidelines on BAP's website on how to prepare a brief practice article so that the focus is relevant to BAP's target audience. BAP has instituted a fast turnaround policy for this type of manuscript such that practitioners can receive current information quickly for integration into practice.

Discussion and/or review paper. Authors of discussion or review papers comment on a topic of interest to the journal's target audience. This manuscript type often involves review of the literature on that topic but is more comprehensive in terms of interpretation and extension. You might find practice models and recommendations under this format, and data are not necessary to submit (though could be a part of this submission type). When little literature exists on a topic, an author might write a discussion or review paper to get ideas going and serve as the basis of future empirical studies on the topic. Common discussion or review paper topics include ethics, supervision, and other professional practice issues.

Brief review. A brief review is a shortened literature review paper that focuses on a specific body of literature. Typically, the journal specifies certain requirements, such as only reviewing literature from a certain time period (e.g., the past five years). These papers are meant to provide readers with a snapshot of a research line and identify areas for future research in a concise manner such that they do not necessarily have to read all articles on a topic. These manuscripts should not be written as a description of each article, but rather should synthesize the literature and add value to what the reader could gain over simply reading all the individual articles on their own.

Literature review. A literature review is a lengthier version of a brief review and typically requires review of all relevant literature on a topic. Like brief reviews, the articles covered should be synthesized. Because a full literature review is lengthier, it allows the author to expand on future directions and discussion of findings.

Replications. Replications are exactly as they sound—replications of existing work already published in the literature. Direct replications are typically accepted and welcomed, though replications and extensions are an acceptable contribution in this category.

Book or product review. A book or product review is also exactly as it sounds—a critique of a book or product in the field of ABA that would help the readers understand more about the book or product from someone intimately familiar with it. Some journals only accept book or product reviews by invitation from the editor. However, other journals will accept this type of manuscript from anyone. Check with the journal first before writing a book or product review.

Calls for Special Issues

Journals will often have a "call for special issues" wherein the editor identifies the need for more literature on a topic and decides to dedicate a full issue of the journal to that topic. In doing so, the editor can invite comments from specific people and allow anyone to submit an article. As an example, in 2020, when COVID-19 impacted the world, behavior analysts were left scurrying to quickly develop resources for families and promote telehealth. Typical service models were altered as restrictions prevented behavior analysts from working as usual. Jonathan Tarbox, the editor of *Behavior Analysis in Practice,* dedicated a special issue to COVID-19 and fast-tracked the peer-review process to get information out to BAP's readership quickly. This special issue contained dozens of articles focused on supporting practitioners in this time of great need. Other special issues have focused on topics such as the mand (*The Analysis of Verbal Behavior*) and supervision (*Behavior Analysis in Practice*). If you have expertise in a particular area of practice, special issues may be particularly appealing to you and could allow a unique avenue in which to publish.

When a special issue is announced, behavior analysts typically share this information via email and the call for papers is posted on the journal's website and through social media channels. Check these sources for up-to-date information on journals and upcoming special issues. Pay attention to deadlines—because all of the work must be published in the same issue, the deadlines are often inflexible, and manuscripts must be submitted on time to get published in the special issue.

Roles

It is important to understand the different roles people play in journals so that you can effectively navigate the publication process.

Editor-in-chief. Every journal has an editor-in-chief, generally referred to as the editor. This position can be paid or unpaid and often rotates every two to four years. Editors of journals are often more senior in the field and have contributed to the literature broadly and contributed specifically to the journal for which they serve as editor. They have often served in other roles before for one or more journals, including serving as an associate editor (described below), on the editorial board, and as a reviewer. Editors are chosen by a board or review panel and are self-nominated or nominated by peers if they meet certain criteria. The editor is ultimately responsible for the journal, its content, and final publication of issues and manuscripts within those issues. The editor has some creative ability to construct special issues, add additional manuscript types, and add issues to the year's publication plan. When you submit to a journal, you always submit directly to the editor-in-chief, who will manage your manuscript, often by assigning it to an associate editor.

Associate editor. Each journal has a group of associate editors (AEs). Depending on the size of the journal, there could be anywhere from two to eight AEs. This is typically an unpaid or minimally paid position and granted to people who have served on editorial boards and as reviewers and have contributed their own work. An AE position typically last two to three years, after which the AE typically rotates off the board, although some AEs can serve multiple terms, and some go on to serve as editor of the journal. The AE's job is to choose a panel of reviewers to review each manuscript they are assigned to. AEs also review the manuscript themselves, review comments from the review panel, and then make a recommendation to the editor about a decision. Ultimately the editor has the final say on whether a manuscript gets accepted for publication, but they often support the recommendation of the AE. AEs typically represent different profiles (e.g., practitioners, academics) and have varied areas of expertise. This diversity allows the editor to choose an appropriate AE for different types of manuscripts, one whose expertise will match the content of the paper.

Editorial board. There are typically dozens of editorial board members, though there could be fewer if the journal is small. Editorial board members typically serve a two- to three-year term and are expected to review a specified number of manuscripts per year. They also are often expected to contribute to the journal through authoring at least one manuscript per year, though this requirement can vary by journal. When an AE receives a manuscript, they will often consider all the editorial board members and identify a group of reviewers who have expertise on that topic. The AE will then assign the manuscript to those reviewers, asking for written feedback and a recommendation on a decision. Not every person who reviews a manuscript must be from the editorial board, but journals usually have a requirement that at least one person be from the editorial board. Editorial boards are often diverse groups of individuals with different areas of expertise who have contributed to the literature in some way. Some editorial board members may go on to serve as AEs.

Reviewer. Reviewers are people in the field. Anyone can serve as a reviewer, and typically an AE identifies a reviewer as someone who could offer a valuable opinion on a manuscript. It is not uncommon for an AE to choose one or two editorial board members and one or two reviewers outside of the board to review a manuscript. Some reviewers go on to be on editorial boards, though some never do.

Guest editor or guest associate editor. Journal editors often provide opportunities for individuals to serve as "guest" editors or AEs. This is done for a few reasons. First, the individual has expertise that the current editor or AE group does not have—so they are asked to manage a certain manuscript or issue of a journal. Second, the individual may be given the opportunity to serve in that role to determine if they may be interested in and be a good fit for a permanent position later down the line. Finally, sometimes guests are past editors or past AEs who are brought in for extra support or expertise.

Editorial assistant. Some journals have an editorial assistant, who can be a graduate student or a full-time professional. Their job is to provide support to the editor in processing manuscripts and managing the details of the publication process.

Here is a flowchart of how the different roles in a journal work together to manage a manuscript from beginning to end:

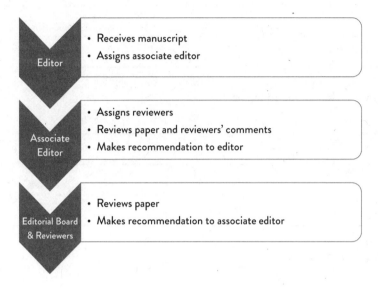

Editor
- Receives manuscript
- Assigns associate editor

Associate Editor
- Assigns reviewers
- Reviews paper and reviewers' comments
- Makes recommendation to editor

Editorial Board & Reviewers
- Reviews paper
- Makes recommendation to associate editor

Blind Submissions

The final detail for you to be knowledgeable about is whether the journal uses single-blind or double-blind reviews. Single-blind reviews mean that the reviewer's identity is kept confidential from the authors. So the authors will see comments, but they will not know who made those comments. The AE's identity is known (for obvious reasons, they need to communicate directly with the authors to support them through the publication process). Double-blind means that the identity of both the authors and the reviewers is kept confidential. Additionally, a journal can choose to have no blinding at all, in which case all identities are revealed. There are disadvantages and advantages to each of these options. The important consideration for you is to decide what you feel most comfortable with. If a journal does not have blind procedures in place, you can ask for single-or double-blind procedures to review your manuscript, and most journals will oblige.

As you can see, there are many factors for you to consider when identifying a journal to submit your manuscript to. If you are at a point in your research journey where you might be ready to choose a journal, take a few moments to answer the following questions to guide your decision. If you are not quite there yet, review these questions and answer them when you are ready to make this decision.

What type of article is this? Data based? Conceptual? Practice oriented?

_____

_____

_____

Whom do I want this article to impact?

_____

_____

_____

_____

Describe the ideal reader of this article.

_____

_____

_____

_____

Describe what you want the reader to know or accomplish after having read your article.

_____

_____

_____

_____

Is there a special issue this manuscript might fit well in?

_____

_____

_____

_____

Now, use this information to review some journals and decide which journal is the best match in terms of its mission, target audience, and types of articles accepted.

Submitting a Manuscript

Now that you've done some preliminary research and have an idea of which journal you will submit to, you are ready to submit your manuscript. Sounds easy, right? Unfortunately, it can be a bit more complicated than it seems. There are some rules you will need to follow while preparing your manuscript for submission, waiting for a response, and responding to the decision. I will walk you through each of these steps here.

How to Prepare Your Manuscript for Submission

Every journal will have specifications on how you should prepare your manuscript prior to submission. Visit the journal's website to find this information. It will almost always be provided in a section called "submit a manuscript" or "submission guidelines for authors." You will see guidance such as deidentification procedures, the format to use for submitting graphs and other visuals, and word requirements. The journal will often describe its editorial procedure, your ethical responsibilities as the author, and any policies or procedures related to data storage, conflicts of interest, and informed consent. This information can often be found directly on the journal's homepage.

Review this content for the journal you've chosen with your manuscript in hand and ensure it meets all the requirements specified by the journal. The last thing you want to do is work hard to submit your manuscript, only to get it bounced back for changes shortly after submission (this has happened to me several times!).

Authorship

Ideally, you will discuss the order of authorship at the initiation of the research study. The first author generally has the most influence over the paper (e.g., had the idea, did most of the work, organized the group), followed by second author, third author, and so on. Having this conversation early on helps prevent hard feelings (e.g., someone thought they would have a higher authorship level than they did) and helps group members steer their efforts appropriately. It is always okay to change authorship throughout the process, and this can be accomplished by having a simple conversation. If you did not have an authorship conversation early on, have it as soon as possible either in person or via phone. I do not recommend discussing this via email unless you have a very good relationship with the coauthors and the authorship is very clear. This is because tone and intent can get lost in email, feelings may be hurt, and confusion may result. In addition to the order of authors, you'll also need to decide on a corresponding author. The corresponding author is the person who will receive the manuscript correspondence from the editor and AE and the person ultimately responsible for submitting the manuscript. When the manuscript is published, the corresponding author will also be the primary point of contact for anyone who wishes to ask questions about the study. The corresponding person can be the same person as the first author, but it does not have to be.

How to Submit Your Manuscript

After you are sure you have met all the journal's specifications, as the corresponding author, you can move on to submitting your manuscript—the exciting part! Most journals have electronic submissions. If you do not already have an account, you will need to create one. Creation of an account is a simple process that requires you to provide basic demographic information and to create a username and password. Once you've created an account, you will need to complete the process of submitting the manuscript. Within the journal's submission system, you will have an option to click "submit a manuscript." After clicking this, you'll be guided through multiple questions and will upload your manuscript. For many journals, you will separate the title page from the main body of the manuscript and from figures, tables, and appendices, uploading them as separate documents. You'll be asked to complete information such as coauthor full names and affiliations, whether you received funding for your work, and any suggestions you may have on AE assignment and/or reviewers for your paper. You will also need to include several statements, such as declarations related to ethics and conflicts of interest. While journals may vary in their requirements, here are some of the most common:

- **Funding**—have you or any of the authors on the paper received funding for this work? If so, from whom and how much?

- **Conflicts of interest**—Do you or any of the authors on the paper have any known conflicts of interest? If so, who does and what are they?

- **Ethics involving human participants**—if human participants are included, you have followed all research ethical guidelines and obtained appropriate informed consent.

- **Author's contributions**—an attestation that the authors listed on the paper have contributed to the paper's conception and design.

You will also be given the opportunity to write to the editor; I highly recommend formulating a letter to the editor that is intentional and professional. You should also include a statement that the work is not and will not be reviewed by any other journal during the submission consideration process for that journal. Here is an example of a cover letter:

Amber Valentino
Address

Dr. Editor

Editor, Popular Behavior Analytic Journal
123 Smith Street
Nowhere, New York 12345

April 13, 2010

Dear Dr. Editor:

I am submitting the brief report entitled "Use of the cues-pause-point procedure to decrease echolalia and increase correct intraverbal responses in a child with autism" for review and possible publication as a brief report in the *Popular Behavior Analytic Journal*. This manuscript has not been previously published and has not, nor will be, submitted for review or publication with another publication outlet during the review process.

Please address all correspondence to me using the information provided below.

Sincerely,

Amber Valentino, Psy.D., BCBA-D

        After you've completed all the fields and uploaded all relevant documents, you hit "submit"! You should immediately receive an email confirming receipt of your manuscript. If you do not, you can always follow up with the editor via email to ensure it has been received. Save this email for future reference—you'll get a numerical assignment that you will use to correspond about your manuscript in the future.

What Happens After Submission

        You wait…and then, you wait some more! The editorial process can be long. After your manuscript is submitted, the editor will review it and assign an AE. Then, the AE will review it and assign reviewers. These parties may not complete this task right away, so several days can pass before action occurs. It also takes some time for reviewers to accept or decline the opportunity to review. If they do decline, the AE must choose new reviewers. Then, the AE gives the reviewers time to complete and upload their reviews. In very short timelines (e.g., brief practices published in BAP), reviewers have only ten days to read the article and submit their decision. In other situations, they may have upward of thirty days. Of course, not all reviewers will meet these deadlines, so the AE must simply wait until all reviews are in.

Once all reviews are in, the AE then reviews those comments, reads the paper in full, makes a decision, and writes a letter. The AE may be managing several other manuscripts and likely a full-time job atop personal responsibilities, so the process understandably is lengthy. You could wait upward of six to eight months to hear anything back. So, what should you do while waiting? I recommend beginning work on another project, or if you feel the need to do so, take a much-needed break! Or do both—take a break, then work on your next project. There really isn't anything you can do on your submitted manuscript while you await a decision, so this is often the perfect excuse to move on to the next project on your list. You are welcome to check in with the editor on occasion if you want an update, but you can also log in to your account on the journal's website, where most online systems will provide a status (e.g., reviewers assigned) so you have a general idea of what's going on.

One important thing you should do while waiting is communicate with your coauthors. Though they will likely get an email confirming the original submission, after that, the primary communication will come from you as the corresponding author. I recommend setting a date on your calendar (perhaps monthly) to send your coauthors a note informing them of the status (e.g., "Wanted to let you know I checked the website today and our manuscript is still under review—keep you posted!"), something simple to keep them engaged and aware that you are managing your responsibility as corresponding author and taking it seriously.

Types of Decisions

There are several decisions that can be made about your manuscript—some of them are easy to understand, whereas for others you may need a bit more information about what they mean and how to respond. Here are the most common types of decisions and what they mean:

Accept. This decision means that your paper has been accepted as is. This is a rare decision because most manuscripts need at least some light editing before publication, but this decision is sometimes made.

Accept pending revisions. This decision means that your paper has been accepted but needs revisions. These can be light editorial revisions or significant revisions. However, your paper will not need to go back out to a new review committee. You might go through multiple rounds of revisions with the AE prior to receiving a final "accept" decision. Editing a manuscript multiple times is a good thing—it means the AE is providing a lot of feedback and detail in revising your manuscript. Thus, you can be confident that when it goes to press, it is polished, with little to no editorial errors.

Reject and resubmit (sometimes called revise and resubmit). This decision means that your paper has been rejected but the journal will consider it again for publication if you are willing to make significant revisions. Once you make those revisions, the paper will go back out to a review panel. Sometimes reviewers from the original panel will serve again, and sometimes the review panel will be completely new. Most often, it is a combination of new reviewers and old ones. You will most likely have the same AE for each revision, unless either party requests a change or, for some reason, the AE is unavailable. The type of revisions requested can vary—from regraphing your data, to collecting data on more participants, to reorganizing and rewriting several sections. Ultimately, you get to decide whether you want to make those changes or not.

Reject. This decision means that your manuscript has been rejected from the journal and cannot be resubmitted. Manuscripts get rejected for a variety of reasons, including a poor fit for the journal, conceptual flaws, poor demonstration of experimental control, or inability of the paper to contribute to the literature on that topic.

What to Do After You Receive a Decision

Luckily, there is action you can take after each decision to hopefully get your paper published.

Accept. This is the easiest decision! Your next steps will be to proofread the article, transfer the copyrights, order any reprints you wish to have (usually for a small fee), and respond to any final inquiries from the editor or publisher.

Accept pending revisions. Your next steps will be to make any changes the AE has recommended. This will involve reviewing the AE's letter and reviewer comments and responding appropriately. Most AEs will ask you to write a response letter outlining how you have addressed each issue. Be sure to inquire about a deadline—most deadlines are about thirty days from the date the decision was received, but some journals may allow more or less time. If you need an extension due to the extent of changes required, you can reach out to the AE to ask for one—they are typically very willing to grant the extension.

Reject and resubmit (or revise and resubmit). After receiving this decision, you'll need to start working through the changes. There are likely to be substantial changes needed, so you should treat this task like any other—break it down via a task analysis and include small, measurable goals. Some goals may be best accomplished by your coauthors, whereas others you will specifically take on. It is best to call a meeting with your coauthors to discuss an action plan and assign responsibilities and deadlines. Take note of the journal's deadline. Some journals may default to a thirty-day resubmission date. This may be doable if the changes are editorial in nature. However, if you must go back and collect more data or substantially change the manuscript, you may need to ask for more time. Make all the changes requested of you and write a cover letter informing the AE how you addressed those changes. If there are any changes you were unable to make or did not agree with, make a note of those and describe them, along with the reason, to the AE. When you have completed the changes, resubmit the manuscript for a second consideration.

Reject. While this is often disappointing, you should think of it as an opportunity to learn and develop your research skills. When a manuscript is rejected from a journal, you cannot submit that manuscript to that journal again. However, you can submit it to a different journal. Review the AE and reviewers' comments and decide if you want to proceed with submitting it to a different journal. You may feel that the review panel has brought critical considerations to your attention that lessen your confidence in the paper, and thus you may choose not to pursue publication. If this is your choice, review everything and take some notes about how you will improve your research in the future based on the feedback you have received. If you decide to submit your manuscript to a different journal, follow the steps in this chapter on choosing a journal, incorporate changes from the review panel and AE of the previous journal, and resubmit your manuscript.

Often the reviewers and AE give you such great feedback that when you incorporate that feedback, your manuscript improves significantly, such that it gets accepted to a different journal. This has happened to me several times! The number of times you submit a manuscript to different journals is totally up to you—there are no rules. I have ranged from one submission to five! One of two things is likely to occur: either (1) the article will get accepted or (2) you will lose momentum after a certain number of rejections and decide to move on. If the latter is the case, do not get discouraged! Every great researcher has multiple manuscripts that never get published. Use this as an opportunity to learn something new to make you a better researcher in the future. I encourage people to continue to try at least a few times for publication. It is possible the first journal you chose has a very high rejection rate, or that you chose a journal that just wasn't a great match for your work. These are things that can be overcome—at the end of the day, you have data and a story to share and you should do your best to find the right outlet in which to share it. Indeed, publishing can be a test of how resistant your behavior is to extinction—so try to persist. It will get easier over time, as you learn which journals are best matches and your writing and research behavior improves. Even the most senior researchers in our field still get manuscripts rejected regularly—this will always be a part of your research career, but one to embrace and use to your advantage.

Appendix D contains examples of response letters to the AE for the "reject with invitation to resubmit" decision and the "accept with revisions" decision—the two categories for which you would need to write a response letter. You can use these sample letters to get an idea of the level of detail to put in your response and use some of the wording to get you started on your own letter.

Finally, to further support you in the publication process, I've provided a diagram of the above steps, which you can use as you navigate submission of your first manuscripts.

Find Journal Requirements	• Edit your manuscript • Write a cover letter to the editor • Submit your manuscript
Wait for a Decision	• Stay in communication with your coauthors • Follow up with the editor occasionally
Receive & Act upon Decision	• <u>Accept</u>: Celebrate and complete final proofing/permissions • <u>Accept with revisions</u>: Make all changes and submit by deadline • <u>Reject with invitation to resubmit</u>: Make changes and resubmit by deadline • <u>Reject</u>: Decide if you'd like to submit to different journal • If you do resubmit, make changes, submit to different journal

Essential Takeaways

To summarize, the editorial process can be a bit daunting! Understanding the timelines and different decisions you may receive can be immensely helpful in approaching the process with confidence and setting expectations appropriately. I hope this chapter has provided you with a framework for the editorial process and knowledge of the people, decisions, and resources available to you to be successful.

Putting It All Together

This book has taken you on a journey from simply wanting to conduct research to having the tools to do it! The chapters in this book follow a natural progression in the research process—from discovering your skills and needs, identifying your motivation, and recognizing your role in research to obtaining mentorship, writing, and navigating the publication process. Now, the task is in your hands. You have the tools necessary to support your ongoing research journey and you have practical, objective tasks to complete to get started on creating and maintaining a research career. Remember, start small and set yourself up for success by choosing achievable and interesting goals. Happy researching!

Resources

To conclude, I provide you with a comprehensive list of resources in various categories. Some of these resources I mentioned throughout the book, whereas others are new. As you consider your professional development and learning, reference this information to find specific resources to assist you in your research journey. Good luck! The journey is an exciting and fruitful one, and one you deserve to take. Pick up your laptop, put on your research hat, and have some ABA research fun!

ABA Journals/Professional Organizations

All ABAI Special Interest Groups (SIGS)
The Association for Behavior Analysis International (ABAI) has several special interest groups (SIGs). These SIGS are open to members of ABAI and are often led by experts in that area. Joining a SIG or two can be a great way to network, learn more about a topic, and get involved. The full list of SIGs can be located here: https://www.abainternational.org/constituents/special-interests/special-interest-groups.aspx

Behavior Analysis in Practice (BAP)
The journal *Behavior Analysis in Practice* (BAP) is a peer-reviewed journal, published quarterly. It is targeted toward practitioners and has several options for manuscript types. The journal "promotes empirically validated best practices in an accessible format that describes what works and the challenges of implementation in practical settings." https://www.abainternational.org/journals.aspx

Journal of Applied Behavior Analysis (JABA)
The *Journal of Applied Behavior Analysis* (JABA) has a long history in our field and is a very prestigious journal to publish in. It is published quarterly and "publishes research about applications of the experimental analysis of behavior to problems of social importance." https://www.onlinelibrary.wiley.com/journal/19383703

The Analysis of Verbal Behavior (TAVB)
The journal *The Analysis of Verbal Behavior* (TAVB) focuses on "the dissemination of innovative empirical research, theoretical conceptualizations, and real-world applications of the behavioral science of language." It is published twice per year. https://www.springer.com/journal/40616

Journal of Organizational Behavior Management (JOBM)
The focus of the *Journal of Organizational Behavior Management* (JOBM) is "scientific prin-
ciples to improve organizational performance through behavior change. The journal publishes research and review articles, reports from the field, discussions, and book reviews on
the topics that are critical to today's organizational development practitioners, operations
managers, and human resource professionals." https://www.tandfonline.com/loi/worg20

California Association for Behavior Analysis (CalABA)
Most states have a professional association, and some have an annual conference. It is worth
examining the professional association in your state and getting involved to access opportunities for mentoring, networking, and learning. CalABA is the largest state association organization in our field and offers an excellent, diverse conference each year. Even if you do not
live in California, it may be worth attending for networking and learning purposes. https://
calaba.org/

Ethics

BACB Professional and Ethical Compliance Code for Behavior Analysts
The Behavior Analyst Certification Board (BACB) created and updates a code of conduct
for professional behavior analysts. The Code contains important guidance for conducting
research as well as practicing ethically as a behavior analyst. https://www.bacb.com/wp
-content/uploads/2020/05/BACB-Compliance-Code-english_190318.pdf

LeBlanc, Nosik, & Petursdottir (2018)
These authors published a paper that provides great guidance for setting up a research review
committee within your organization. The paper can be accessed through a subscription to
the journal it was published in, BAP. The full citation is LeBlanc, L. A., Nosik, M. R., &
Petursdottir, A. (2018). Establishing consumer protections for research in human service
agencies. *Behavior Analysis in Practice, 11,* 445–455. https://doi.org/10.1007/s40617-018
-0206-3

ABAI Ethics Special Interest Group (SIG)
As mentioned above, ABAI has several special interest groups, and this one might be worth
joining if you are interested in publishing on the topic of ethics. You can find this SIG and
information about how to join it here: https://www.abainternational.org/constituents/special
-interests/special-interest-groups.aspx)

Bailey & Burch's *Ethics for Behavior Analysts*
This book about ethics is very well cited and widely used by behavior analysis professionals.
It is a helpful resource generally, but a must have if you are interested in publishing on
the topic of ethics.

Mentoring and Networking

National Mentoring Resource Center - https://nationalmentoringresourcecenter.org/
This website provides numerous materials related to mentoring, including training, blogs, programs, best practices, and other learning opportunities. Though not specifically related to the field of behavior analysis, it can be a valuable resource for individuals wishing to get involved in mentoring experiences.

Women in Behavior Analysis (WIBA) - https://www.thebaca.com/about-wiba/
WIBA's mission is to empower, celebrate, and mentor women behavior analysts. They hold an annual conference that may be valuable to individuals seeking mentorship.

Becerra, Sellers, & Contreras (2020)
The article titled "Maximizing the Conference Experience: Tips to Effectively Navigate Academic Conferences Early in Professional Careers," published in BAP, is the first of its kind to offer practical guidance to conference goers on how to get the most out of the conference experience—from choosing the right conference, to attending, to networking and follow-up. You can access this article through a subscription to the journal BAP.

Public Speaking

Friman (2014)
Pat Friman is a well-known behavior analyst, noted for his excellent public speaking skills. In 2014, he wrote an article that is well cited in the behavior analytic public speaking arena titled "Behavior Analysts to the Front! A 15-Step Tutorial on Public Speaking." The article is extremely well written and offers practical guidance on developing public speaking skills. You can access it through the journal *The Behavior Analyst*, which is free to members of the Association for Behavior Analysis International (ABAI).

Heinicke, Juanico, Valentino, & Sellers (in press)
These authors systematically interviewed the top public speakers in our field for their article "Improving Behavior Analysts' Public Speaking: Recommendations from Expert Interviews," published in *Behavior Analysis in Practice*. The paper provides practical tips and strategies based on what these experts do to have such effective public speaking skills. Use this paper in conjunction with Friman's paper to get a variety of ideas on how to improve your public speaking throughout your professional career.

"How to speak so that people want to listen"
This short TED talk by Julian Treasure in 2013 provides simple tips via the acronym HAIL (Honesty, Authenticity, Integrity, and Love) on how to speak and have influence. It can be accessed here: https://www.ted.com/talks/julian_treasure_how_to_speak_so_that_people _want_to_ listen?language=en

TED Talks

Watching TED Talks generally is a great place to observe models for public speaking. Of course, some speakers are better than others, but TED Talk speakers have rules regarding use of visuals such as PowerPoint slides and reading text. Thus, most TED Talks are very good and provide models for how to present eloquently. They are also very short, making them easy to view during brief breaks from work or other downtime. You can observe many TED Talks and take note of what you like in a speaker versus what you do not, trying to imitate those behaviors that seem most influential to you as a listener. The bonus is that you will learn something along the way in addition to seeing great public speaking models. You can access thousands of TED Talks on a variety of topics here: https://www.ted.com

Research to Practice/Accessing Literature

Valentino & Juanico (2020)

I referenced this article several times in my book because it was the impetus for writing more about this topic. My coauthor, Jessica, and I were very interested in the research-to-practice gap and identifying the barriers that exist for practitioners conducting research in applied settings. We both had strong research careers throughout our practice but had to overcome several barriers ourselves to achieve this (and still struggle with many). We wondered if other practitioners faced the same barriers, and we felt motivated to assess this as well as offer recommendations about how we were able to overcome them. The paper is titled "Overcoming Barriers to Applied Research: A Guide for Practitioners" and can be accessed in the journal *Behavior Analysis in Practice.*

Kelley, Wilder, Carr, Ray, Green, & Lipschultz (2015)

This was one of the first articles on the research-to-practice gap to come out and offered some excellent suggestions, based on interviews with prolific practitioner-researchers, for getting involved and staying productive. The title of the article is "Research Productivity Among Practitioners in Behavior Analysis: Recommendations from the Prolific" and can be accessed via the journal *Behavior Analysis in Practice.*

Carr & Briggs (2010)

This article provides practical strategies to practitioners about how to maintain contact with the scholarly literature after graduation. Although a bit dated, many of the suggestions still apply and are useful to implement. The article, titled "Strategies for Making Contact with the Scholarly Literature," can be accessed via the journal *Behavior Analysis in Practice.*

The PartnerShip (https://www.baresearchcitations.com/)

This is a great website dedicated to bridging the gap between research and practice. A research team at The PartnerShip browses the literature, and they provide the article title, abstract, and full article if it is available for free. They send a monthly newsletter summarizing recently published key articles. For a small annual subscription, you can get additional support locating articles that are difficult to find.

Supervision

Fieldwork and Supervision for Behavior Analysts: A Handbook

This book by Brian Rice, Ellie Kazemi, and Peter Adzhyan provides practical guidance for navigating the fieldwork and supervision experience, as well as worksheets and handouts to use along the way.

Here is a full list of articles, chapters, and books you can read on the topic of supervision:

Agnew, T., Vaught, C., Getz, H., & Fortune, J. (2000). Peer group clinical supervision program fosters confidence and professionalism. *Professional School Counseling, 4*, 6–12.

Barnes-Holmes, D. (2018). A commentary on the student-supervisor relationship: A shared journey of discovery. *Behavior Analysis in Practice, 11*(2), 174–176. https://doi.org/10.1007/s40617-018-0227-y

Behavior Analyst Certification Board (2012). *Supervisor training curriculum outline.*

Cavalari, R. N. S., Gillis, J. M., Kruser, N., & Romanczyk, R. G. (2015). Digital communication and records in service provision and supervision: Regulation and practice. *Behavior Analysis in Practice, 8*(2), 176–189. https://doi.org/10.1007/s40617-014-0030-3

Chang, J. (2012). A contextual-functional meta-framework for counselling supervision. *International Journal for the Advancement of Counselling, 2*, 71–87. https://doi.org/10.1007/s10447-012-9168-2

Clark, H. B., Wood, R., Kuehnel, T., Flanagan, S., Mosk, M., & Northrup, J. T. (2008). Preliminary validation and training of supervisory interactional skills. *Journal of Organizational Behavior Management, 7*, 95–116. https://doi.org/10.1300/J075v07n01_07

Conners, B., Johnson, A., Duarte, J., Murriky, R., & Marks, K. (2019). Future directions of training and fieldwork in diversity issues in applied behavior analysis. *Behavior Analysis in Practice.* https://doi.org/10.1007/s40617-019-00349-2

Daniels, J., D'Andrea, M., & Kim, B. S. (1999). Assessing the barriers and changes of cross-cultural supervision: A case study. *Counselor Education and Supervision, 38*, 191–204. https://doi.org/10.1002/j.1556-6978.1999.tb00570.x

DiGennero, F. D., & Henley, A. J. (2015). A survey of staff training and performance management practices: The good, the bad, and the ugly. *Behavior Analysis in Practice, 8*, 16–26. https://doi.org/10.1007/s40617-015-0044-5

Dillon, M. J., Kent, H. M., & Malott, R. M. (2008). A supervisory system for accomplishing long-range projects: An application to master's thesis research. *Journal of Organizational Behavior Management, 2*, 213–227. https://doi.org/10.1300/J075v02n03_07

Dixon, D. R., Linstead, E., Granpeesheh, D., Novack, M.N., French, R., Stevens, E., Stevens, L., & Powell, A. (2016). An evaluation of the impact of supervision intensity, supervisor qualifications, and caseload on outcomes in the treatment of autism spectrum disorder. *Behavior Analysis Practice, 9*(4), 339–348. https://doi.org/10.1007/s40617-016-0132-1

Dubuque, E. M., & Dubuque, M. L. (2018). Guidelines for the establishment of a university-based practical training system. *Behavior Analysis in Practice, 11*(1), 51–61. https://doi.org/10.1007/s40617-016-0154-8

Fleming, R. K., Oliver, J. R., & Bolton, D. M. (1996). Training supervisors to train staff: A case study in a human service organization. *Journal or Organizational Behavior Management, 16,* 3–25.

Fong, E. H., Catagnus, R. M., Brodhead, M., Quigley, S., & Field, S. (2016). Developing the cultural awareness skills of behavior analysts. *Behavior Analysis in Practice, 9,* 84–94. https://doi.org/10.1007/s40617-016-0111-6

Garza, K. L., McGee, H. M., Schenk, Y. A., & Wiskirchen, R. R. (2018). Some tools for carrying out a proposed process for supervising experience hours for aspiring board certified behavior analysts. *Behavior Analysis in Practice, 11*(1), 62–70. https://doi.org/10.1007/s40617-017-0186-8

Hartley, B. K., Courtney, W. T., Rosswurm, M., & LaMarca, V. L. (2016). The apprentice: An innovative approach to meet the Behavior Analyst Certification Board's supervision standards. *Behavior Analysis in Practice, 9*(4), 329–338.

Holley, W. (2005). Supervision: Using the evidence to support our practice. *Kairaranga, 6,* 41–48.

Hulse, D., & Robert, T. (2014). Preplanning for feedback in clinical supervision: Enhancing readiness for feedback exchange. *The Journal for Counselor Preparation and Supervision, 6*(2). https://doi.org/10.7729/62.1091

LeBlanc, L. A., Heinicke, M. R., & Baker, J. C. (2012). Expanding the consumer base for behavior-analytic services: Meeting the needs in the 21st century. *Behavior Analysis in Practice, 5*(1), 4–14.

LeBlanc, L. A., & Luiselli, J. K. (2016). Refining supervisory practices in the field of behavior analysis: Introduction to the special section on supervision. *Behavior Analysis in Practice, 9*(4), 271–273. https://doi.org/10.1007/s40617-016-0156-6

Mason, L. L., Perales, J., & Gallegos, E. (2013). Community-based development of rural behavior analysts. *Rural Special Education Quarterly, 32*(3), 20–23.

Morgan, M. M., & Sprenkle, D. H. (2007). Toward a common-factors approach to supervision. *Journal of Marital and Family Therapy, 33,* 1–17.

Palmer-Olsen, P., Gold, L. L., & Woolley, S. R. (2011). Supervising emotionally focused therapists: A systematic research-based model. *Journal of Marital and Family Therapy, 37,* 411–426.

Parsons, M. B., Rollyson, J. H., Iverson, J., & Reid, D. H. (2012). Evidence-based staff training: A guide for practitioners. *Behavior Analysis in Practice, 5*(2), 2–11.

Pilgrim, C. (2018). Some thoughts on shaping future behavior analysts: A call to stay true to our roots. *Behavior Analysis in Practice, 11,* 204–205. https://doi.org/10.1007/s40617-018-0233-0

Reid, D. H., Parsons, M. B., & Green, C. W. (2012). *The supervisor's guidebook: Evidence-based strategies for promoting work quality and enjoyment among human service staff.* Habilitative Management Consultants.

Reid, D. H., & Green, C. W. (1990). Staff training. In J. L. Matson (Ed.), *Handbook of behavior modification with the mentally retarded* (2nd ed., pp. 71–90). Plenum Press.

Reid, D. H., Parsons, M. B., Lattimore, L. P., Towery, D. L., & Reade, K. K. (2005). Improving staff performance through clinician application of outcome management. *Research in Developmental Disabilities, 26,* 101–116.

Reid, D. H., Rotholz, D. A., Parsons, M. B., Morris, L., Braswell, B. A., Green, C. W., & Schell, R. M. (2003). Training human service supervisors in aspects of PBS: Evaluation of a statewide, performance-based program. *Journal of Positive Behavior Interventions, 5,* 35–46.

Schepis, M. M., & Reid, D. H. (1994). Training direct service staff in congregate settings to interact with people with severe disabilities: A quick, effective and acceptable program. *Behavioral Interventions, 9,* 13–26.

Shuler, N., & Carroll, R.A., (2018). Training supervisors to provide performance feedback using video modeling with voiceover instructions. *Behavior Analysis in Practice, 12*(3), 576–591. https://doi.org/10.1007/s40617-018-00314-5

Sellers, T. P., Alai-Rosales, S., & MacDonald, R. P. (2016a). Taking full responsibility: The ethics of supervision in behavior analytic practice. *Behavior Analysis in Practice, 9,* 299–308. https://doi.org/10.1007/s40617-016-0144-x

Sellers, T. P., Valentino, A. L., & LeBlanc, L. A. (2016b). Recommended practices for individual supervision of aspiring behavior analysts. *Behavior Analysis in Practice, 9*(4), 274–286. https://doi.org/10.1007/s40617-016-0110-7

Sellers, T. P, Valentino, A. L., Landon, T., & Aielo, S. (2019). Board Certified Behavior Analysts' supervisory practices: Survey results and recommendations. *Behavior Analysis in Practice, 12*(3), 536–546. https://doi.org/10.1007/s40617-019-00367-0

Sellers, T. P., LeBlanc, L. A., & Valentino, A. L. (2016). Recommendations for detecting and addressing barriers to successful supervision. *Behavior Analysis in Practice, 9*(4), 309–319. https://doi.org/10.1007/s40617-016-0142-z

Subramaniam, A., Silong, A.D., & Ismail, I. A. (2015). Effects of coaching supervision, mentoring supervision, and abusive supervision on talent development among trainee doctors in public hospitals: Moderating role of clinical learning environment. *Medical Education, 15,* 129–137. https://doi.org/10.1186/s12909-015-0407-1

Turner, L. B., Fischer, A. J., & Luiselli, J. K. (2016). Towards a competency-based, ethical and socially valid approach to the supervision of applied behavior analytic trainees. *Behavior Analysis in Practice, 9*(4), 287–298. https://doi.org/10.1007/s40617-016-0121-4

Valentino, A. L., LeBlanc, L. A., & Sellers, T. P. (2016). The benefits of group supervision and a recommended structure for implementation. *Behavior Analysis in Practice, 9*(4), 320–328. https://doi.org/10.1007/s40617-016-0138-8

Valentino, A. L. (in press). Supervision and mentoring. In J. Luiselli, R. M. Gardner, F. L. Bird, & H. Maguire (Eds.), *Organizational Behavior Management (OBM) Approaches for Intellectual and Developmental Disabilities.*

Time Management

How to Write a Lot: A Practical Guide to Productive Academic Writing (2nd ed.), by **Paul Silvia**

It may seem odd that I am putting this resource under the time management section! While it is a great book for learning some writing skills, it's also an amazing resource for time management, specific to writing and research behavior. I reference it several times in this book. For me, this read was quite behavior altering—I changed the way I scheduled, thought about, and completed research-related tasks. After following many of the suggestions from Silvia, my productivity skyrocketed, and I was able to accomplish many research-related goals in a very short period of time. It is also a very short read, and one that you can revisit time and time again throughout your career to refresh your approach, time management, and overall thinking related to research productivity.

Essentialism: The Disciplined Pursuit of Less, by **Greg McKeown**

This book helps you to conceptualize what is truly important in your life and then to remove what is not. I loved reading it shortly after having my first child. McKeown does a great job of helping you see how doing less is actually doing more.

Deep Work: Rules for Focused Success in a Distracted World, by **Cal Newport**

This book is a must read for anybody in search of a new time-management philosophy. Newport's concept of "deep work" is highly relevant to research productivity and can be applied easily to your goal of becoming an applied researcher. I consider this book to be in the top three that have influenced my career and productivity. I also purchased his planner and use it religiously to time-block my entire day—and it works!

Getting Things Done: The Art of Stress-Free Productivity, by **David Allen**

This is a very popular book on time management, written by a productivity consultant. Although it is not specific to research and writing, it is a very useful tool for thinking about how best to manage your time to get things done.

Discover Business website: Time Management Guide and Resource

This is a useful guide that I stumbled upon a few years ago and have referenced periodically. It has six chapters, all freely available online. The chapters span topics such as use of technology, modifications to your work environment to promote productivity, and specific behaviors you should engage in to manage your time most effectively. https://www.discover business.us/resources/time-management/

Writing

Purdue Online Writing Lab (OWL)

This is a website through the College of Liberal Arts at Purdue University that hosts several resources and instructional materials on writing. These resources are available for free through the writing lab at Purdue at https://owl.purdue.edu/owl/purdue_owl.html.

The APA Style website

This is a wonderful resource for APA-style writing: https://apastyle.apa.org/

Publication Manual of the American Psychological Association (7th edition, 2020)

Almost all journals will require you to write according to APA style. Every several years, the APA comes out with a new edition of this manual, so you will always want to ensure you have the most recent edition (many guidelines change from edition to edition). It is a pretty large manual with many guidelines, and it is not necessary to memorize everything. Having it at your disposal will help you look things up and review samples so you write according to APA style. With more and more use, you will begin to memorize certain writing conventions.

Acknowledgments

I signed this book contract the day before our son was due. I had no idea what the next year would hold. Everything in life was more challenging yet more rewarding than I ever could have imagined. None of this would have been possible without my husband, **Garth Girman**. Thank you for your never-ending support and encouragement, and of course, for reminding me to eat.

A very special thank you to **Ryan Buresh** and **Caleb Beckwith** at New Harbinger Press. Your vision for this book helped me see the possibilities and helped me to develop the book beyond what I thought it could be. **Rona Bernstein** at PsychEditing—you are a fantastic editor and a pure joy to work with! Thank you for your attention to detail, amazing additions, and teaching me a lot about style!

To **Pat Friman**—Thank you for your encouraging words on an early version of this book and for writing such a thoughtful foreword. You are an inspiration to the field and to me.

This was, indeed, the longest and shortest year of my life. Thank you to **Ned Carlson** for your support of my writing. You're a great boss, most of the time.

Thank you to **Josh Sleeper** for teaching me that eggnog really is one of life's greatest small pleasures.

When I transitioned to Trumpet Behavioral Health in 2012, I thought I would also naturally transition out of applied research. **Linda LeBlanc**, you were not having that. Thank you for encouraging my research career and giving me such great professional opportunities. Thank you for creating the research infrastructure, systems and processes at TBH. The strong foundation of research culture within the company that you created has allowed me and the research culture to thrive over the past decade.

Sarah Trautman, you are an inspiration for entrepreneurship and creativity. I thought of your will, persistence, and focus often while writing this book. You are also my number one Santa-Frenchie-baby picture fan.

As a behavior analyst, some families impact you in ways that change your perspective and the trajectory of your career. **Mu and Feda**—you were that family to me. You inspired some of my applied work. You had an amazingly positive impact. Not just on me, but on the world. You are missed.

To all the crew at **Trumpet Behavioral Health**—I am so proud and honored to be a part of this amazing team. Keep making a difference. Thank you to the TBH leadership team for generously allowing me to share our resources in this book.

To all the families over the years that have given me the opportunity to work with your children. It has been an honor.

Finally, to my son, **Porter Girman**. You are beautiful, intelligent, kind, and funny. As I write, you are thirteen months old. It is 5 a.m. and Daddy is distracting you in the other room while I finish the book in time for my final deadline. Know that you are the best thing that ever happened to me. I hope you read this someday and are inspired. You can do anything you want in life. I love you very much.

References

Aguirre, A. A., Valentino, A. L., & LeBlanc, L. A. (2016). Empirical investigations of the intraverbal: 2005–2015. *The Analysis of Verbal Behavior, 32*(2), 139–153. https://doi.org/10.1007/s40616-016-0064-4

American Psychological Association. (2020). *Publication Manual of the American Psychological Association* (7th ed.).

Anglesea, M., Hoch, H., & Taylor, B. (2008). Reducing rapid eating in teenagers with autism: Use of a pager prompt. *Journal of Applied Behavior Analysis, 41,* 107–111. https://doi.org/10.1901/jaba.2008.41-107

Azrin, N. H., & Foxx, R. M. (1971). A rapid method of toilet training the institutionalized retarded. *Journal of Applied Behavior Analysis, 4,* 89–99.

Becerra, L., Sellers, T., & Contreras, B. (2020). Maximizing the conference experience: Tips to effectively navigate academic conferences early in professional careers. *Behavior Analysis in Practice.* https://doi.org/10.1007/s40617-019-00406-w

Behavior Analyst Certification Board. (2020). *Ethics code for behavior analysts.* Littleton, CO: Author.

Carr, J. E., & Briggs, A. M. (2010). Strategies for making regular contact with the scholarly literature. *Behavior Analysis in Practice, 3,* 13–18. https://doi.org/10.1007/bf03391760

Friman, P. C. (2014). Behavior analysts to the front! A 15-step tutorial on public speaking. *The Behavior Analyst, 37,* 109–118.

Geiger, K. B., Carr, J. C., & LeBlanc, L. A. (2010). Function-based treatments for escape-maintained problem behavior. *Behavior Analysis in Practice, 3,* 22–32.

Green, G. (2001). Behavior analytic instruction for learners with autism: Advances in stimulus control technology. *Focus on Autism and Other Developmental Disabilities, 16*(2), 72–85.

Grow, L., & LeBlanc, L. (2013). Teaching receptive language skills: Recommendations for instructors. *Behavior Analysis in Practice, 6,* 56–75.

Heinicke, M. R., Juanico, J. F., Valentino, A. L. & Sellers, T. P. (in press). Improving behavior analysts' public speaking: Recommendations from expert interviews. *Behavior Analysis in Practice.*

Heinicke, M. R., Carr, J. E., Pence, S. T., Zias, D. R., Valentino, A. L., & Falligant, J. M. (2016). Assessing the efficacy of pictorial preference assessments for children with developmental disabilities. *Journal of Applied Behavior Analysis, 49,* 848–868. https://doi.org/10.1002/jaba.342

Iwata, B. A., Dorsey, M. F., Slifer, K. J., Bauman, K. E., & Richman, G. S. (1994). Toward a functional analysis of self-injury. *Journal of Applied Behavior Analysis, 27,* 197–209. (Reprinted from *Analysis and Intervention in Developmental Disabilities,* 1982, 2, 3–20).

Iwata, B., & Dozier, C. (2008). Clinical application of functional analysis methodology. *Behavior Analysis in Practice, 1,* 3–9.

Jessel, J., Hanley, P., & Ghaemmaghami, M. (2016). Interview-informed synthesized contingency analysis: Thirty replications and reanalysis. *Journal of Applied Behavior Analysis, 49,* 576–595.

Jin, S., & Hanley, G. (2013). An individualized and comprehensive approach to treating sleep problems in young children. *Journal of Applied Behavior Analysis, 46,* 161–180.

Kelley, D. P., Wilder, D. A., Carr, J. E., Ray, C., Green, N., & Lipschultz, J. (2015). Research productivity among practitioners in behavior analysis: Recommendations from the prolific. *Behavior Analysis in Practice, 8,* 201–206. https://doi.org/10.1007/s40617-015-0064-1

Kodak, T., Fuchtman, R., & Paden, A. (2013). A comparison of intraverbal training procedures for children with autism. *Journal of Applied Behavior Analysis, 45,* 155–160.

LeBlanc, L. A., Nosik, M. R., & Petursdottir, A. (2018). Establishing consumer protections for research in human service agencies. *Behavior Analysis in Practice, 11,* 445–455. https://doi.org/10.1007/s40617-018-0206-3

McKeown, G. (2014). *Essentialism: The disciplined pursuit of less.* Crown Business.

McMorrow, M. J., Foxx, R. M., Faw, G. D., & Bittle, R. G. (1987). Cues-pause-point language training: Teaching echolalics functional use of their verbal labeling repertoires. *Journal of Applied Behavior Analysis, 20,* 11–22.

Newport, C. (2016). *Deep Work: Rules for focused success in a distracted world.* Grand Central Publishing.

Rivas, K., Piazza, C., Roane, H., Volkert, V., Stewart, V., Kadey, H., & Groff, R. (2014). Analysis of self-feeding in children with feeding disorders. *Journal of Applied Behavior Analysis, 47,* 710–722.

Rynes, S., Colbert, A., & Brown, K. (2002). HR professionals' belief about effective human resource practices: Correspondence between research and practice. *Human Resource Management, 41,* 149–174. https://doi.org/10.1002/hrm.10029

Sellers, T. P., LeBlanc, L. A., & Valentino, A. L. (2016). Recommendations for detecting and addressing barriers to successful supervision. *Behavior Analysis in Practice, 9*(4), 309–319. https://doi.org/10.1007/s40617-016-0142-z

Sellers, T. P., Valentino, A. L., & LeBlanc, L. A. (2016). Recommended practices for individual supervision of aspiring behavior analysts. *Behavior Analysis in Practice, 9*(4), 274–286. https://doi.org/10.1007/s40617-016-0110-7

Shabani, D. B., Katz, R. C., Wilder, D. A., Beauchamp, K., Taylor, C. R., & Fischer, K. J. (2002). Increasing social initiations in children with autism: Effects of a tactile prompt. *Journal of Applied Behavior Analysis, 35,* 79–83. https://doi.org/10.1901/jaba.2002.35-79

Shillingsburg, M. A., Bowen, C. N. & Valentino, A. L. (2014). Mands for information using "how" under EO-absent and EO-present conditions. *The Analysis of Verbal Behavior, 30,* 54–61. https://doi.org/10.1007/s40616-013-0002-7

Silvia, P. J. (2007). *How to write a lot: A practical guide to productive academic writing.* American Psychological Association.

Taylor, B. A., Hughes, C. E., Richard, E., Hoch, H., & Rodriquez-Coello, A. (2004). Teaching teenagers with autism to seek assistance when lost. *Journal of Applied Behavior Analysis, 37,* 79–82. https://doi.org/10.1901/jaba.2004.37-79

Taylor, B. A., & Levin, L. (1998). Teaching a student with autism to make verbal initiations: Effects of a tactile prompt. *Journal of Applied Behavior Analysis, 31,* 651–654. doi:10.1901/jaba.1998.31-651

Valentino, A. L. (in press). Supervision and mentoring. In J. Luiselli, R. M. Gardner, F. L. Bird, & H. Maguire (Eds.), *Organizational behavior management (OBM) approaches for intellectual and developmental disabilities.*

Valentino, A. L., Brice-Fu, S., & Padover, J. L. (2019). Teaching mands for information using "Why" to children with autism. *The Analysis of Verbal Behavior, 35,* 245–257. https://doi.org/10.1007/s40616-019-00113-1

Valentino, A. L., & Juanico, J. F. (2020). Overcoming barriers to conduct applied research: A guide for practitioners. *Behavior Analysis in Practice, 13*(4), 894–904. https://doi.org/10.1007/s40617-020-00479-y

Valentino, A. L., LeBlanc, L. A., & Raetz, P. B. (2018). Evaluation of stimulus intensity fading on reduction of rapid eating in a child with autism. *Journal of Applied Behavior Analysis, 51*(1), 177–182. https://doi.org/10.1002/jaba.433

Valentino, A. L., LeBlanc, L. A., & Sellers, T. P. (2016). The benefits of group supervision and a recommended structure for implementation. *Behavior Analysis in Practice, 9*(4), 320–328. https://doi.org/10.1007/s40617-016-0138-8

Valentino, A. L., Shillingsburg, M. A., & Call, N. A. (2012). Comparing echoic prompts and echoic prompts plus motor movements on intraverbal behavior. *Journal of Applied Behavior Analysis, 45,* 431–435.

Valentino, A. L., Shillingsburg, M. A., Conine, D. E., & Powell, N. M. (2012). Decreasing echolalia of the instruction "say" through use of the cues-pause-point procedure. *Journal of Behavioral Education, 21,* 315–328.

Veazey, S. E., Valentino, A. L., Low, A. L., McElroy, A. M., & LeBlanc, L. A. (2016). Teaching feminine hygiene skills to young females with autism spectrum disorder and intellectual disability. *Behavior Analysis in Practice, 9* (2), 184–189.

Wandersman, A., Duffy, J., Flaspohler, P., Noonan, R., Lubell, K., Stillman, L., & Saul, J. (2008). Bridging the gap between prevention research and practice: The interactive systems framework for dissemination and implementation. *American Journal of Community Psychology, 41,* 171–181. https://doi.org/10.1007/s10464-008-9174-z

Amber L. Valentino, PsyD, BCBA-D, currently serves as chief clinical officer at Trumpet Behavioral Health. In this role, she oversees all research and training initiatives, builds clinical standards for the organization, and structures systems for high-quality clinical service delivery. Valentino's clinical and research interests include the assessment and treatment of verbal behavior, primarily in children with autism. She is also interested in evaluation of programming to address unique adaptive skill deficits, professional practice issues such as ethics, and developing standards for effective supervision in the field.

Valentino has spent her research career conducting applied studies and publishing in several peer-reviewed behavior analytic journals. She currently serves as an associate editor for *Behavior Analysis in Practice*, and previously served as an associate editor for *The Analysis of Verbal Behavior*. She is on the editorial board of the *Journal of Applied Behavior Analysis*, and serves as a frequent guest reviewer for several behavior analytic journals.

Foreword writer **Patrick C. Friman, PhD, ABPP**, is vice president of behavioral health at Boys Town, and clinical professor in the department of pediatrics at the University of Nebraska School of Medicine. He is a fellow of the Association for Behavior Analysis International, former editor of the *Journal of Applied Behavior Analysis*, and former president of the Association for Behavior Analysis International.

Index

A

about this book, 3–8
accepted manuscripts, 150
accomplishments: regularly reviewing, 115–118; worksheet for identifying, 34–37
accountability in research, 120
accuracy of data: ethics code on, 47–48; scenarios and recommendations, 49–50, 52
acknowledging contributions, 47, 53
Adzhyan, Peter, 159
Allen, David, 162
American Psychological Association (APA), 133
analysis: data, 84–85; functional, 10, 19; task, 78–82
The Analysis of Verbal Behavior (TAVB) journal, 90, 97, 141, 143, 155
annual renewal and review process, 64–66; application example, 66; document example, 65
APA style, 133–134, 163
applications: research renewal, 66; research study, 61
applied behavior analysis (ABA): advancing the field of, 19–22; benefits of published research in, 19–30; journals and professional organizations, 155–156; research-to-practice gap in, 9; unique and individual contributions to, 22–23
approachable writing style, 134
article types, 141–142
associate editors (AEs): guests serving as, 144; revisions required by, 49–50; role description for, 143–144

Association for Behavior Analysis International (ABAI), 155, 156, 157
assumptions, questioning, 39–40
audience: journal readership or, 140; targeting a different, 137
authorship: conversations about, 147–148; levels of, 47; sole, 136–137
autistic individuals: research on verbal behavior in, 103; vibrating pagers used with, 24–25

B

balance, work-life, 76–78
barriers to research, 17, 94–100; definition of obstacles vs., 88; lack of opportunities, 94–95; limited access to literature, 95–100. See also obstacles to research
Behavior Analysis in Practice (BAP) journal, 62, 88, 90, 97, 118, 135, 140, 142, 143, 155
Behavior Analyst Certification Board (BACB), 42, 44, 98, 99, 156
Behavior Analyst journal, 157
benefits of publishing research, 19–43; ABA field benefits, 19–30; personal benefits, 31–42
blind review procedures, 145
blog writing, 137
board-certified behavior analysts (BCBAs), 4–6, 9, 42, 89
book reviews, 142
breaks, writing, 135
brief practice articles, 142
brief reports, 141–142
brief review papers, 142
burnout, 77, 135

C

California Association for Behavior Analysis (CalABA), 156
career boost, publishing as, 33–37
citations, use of, 134
clinical practice: embedding research practices into, 108; identifying research questions through, 104; questioning your assumptions about, 39–40; research leading to improvements in, 37–39
code of ethics, 44–48
company-wide literature request system, 96–98
competence in conducting research: ethics code on, 46; scenario and recommendation, 53
conferences, networking at, 112–113, 157
confidentiality: ethics code on, 45–46; scenario and recommendation, 49
conflicts of interest: ethics code on, 46; journal questions about, 148; scenario and recommendation, 51
consumers, benefits of research for, 24–27
continuing education units (CEUs), 42
corresponding authors, 148
credit, giving appropriate, 47, 53
critical reviews, 136
cues-pause-point procedure, 1, 27
CVs or resumes, 117

D

data: accuracy and use of, 47–48, 50, 52; decision making based on, 84–85; retention of relevant, 47
decision making: data-based, 84–85; research process and, 102–104
Deep Work: Rules for Focused Success in a Distracted World (Newport), 83, 162
Discover Business website, 162
discussion papers, 142
distractions, removing, 105–106
documentation, research, 47
double-blind reviews, 145
downtime, scheduling, 114

E

echoic prompts, 2
editorial assistants, 144
editorial boards, 144
editorial process, 134, 138–153; article types and, 141–142; decision types and, 150–152; journal information and, 138–147; manuscript submission and, 149–150; peer review and, 139; roles of people in, 143–145
editor-in-chief, 143
ego boost, publishing as, 31–33
environment, work, 105–107, 136
Essentialism: The Disciplined Pursuit of Less (McKeown), 78, 162
ethical issues, 44–54; code of ethics for, 44–48; governing bodies for, 55–73; journal requirements and, 148; questions to consider about, 54; real-life situations related to, 89; resources for learning about, 90, 156; scenarios and recommendations on, 48–54
ethical oversight, 55–73; alternative research approaches and, 73; institutional review board for, 55, 72–73; research review committee for, 55–72
Ethics for Behavior Analysts (Bailey & Burch), 90, 156
experimental design, 89

F

fear of making mistakes, 91–93
feedback, incorporating, 136
feeding disorders, 91
field-related research benefits, 19–30; advancement of ABA field, 19–22; help for consumers and general public, 24–27; help for other researchers, 27–28; providing a research role model, 29–30; unique and individual contributions, 22–23
Fieldwork and Supervision for Behavior Analysts: A Handbook (Rice, Kazemi, & Adzhyan), 159

final read through, 134–135
flowcharts: on choosing research topics, 12; on manuscript management, 145
focusing on one project, 86
Friman, Patrick C., ix, 111, 157
fun of research work, 41–42
functional analysis, 10, 19
funding, questions about, 148

G

Getting Things Done: The Art of Stress-Free Productivity (Allen), 162
goal setting: bigger goals and, 119; task analysis and, 79
Google Reader, 95
Google Scholar, 95, 99
guest editors, 144

H

How to Write a Lot (Silvia), 83, 162

I

ideas, generating, 93–94
impact factor, 138–139
imperfection, allowing for, 108–109
informed consent: ethics code on, 45; language for obtaining, 62; scenario and recommendation, 50; template for study-specific, 62–63; training checklist for obtaining, 71–72
institutional review board (IRB): overview description of, 55; utilizing at a university, 72–73
interobserver agreement (IOA) data, 37, 48

J

Journal of Applied Behavior Analysis (JABA), 24, 27, 97, 124, 138, 155
Journal of Organizational Behavior Management (JOBM), 156
journals, 138–147; accessing content in, 95–96; article types accepted by, 141–142; blind procedures of, 145; impact factor of, 138–139; list of ABA, 155–156; manuscript decisions from, 150–152;

mission statement of, 140–141; peer-review process of, 139; questions for choosing, 145–146; readership or audience of, 140; roles of people producing, 143–145; special issues of, 143; submission of manuscripts to, 147–150
Juanico, Jessica, 88

K

Kazemi, Ellie, 159
keywords, 79, 80, 99, 100
knowledge, lack of, 88–91

L

laws, complying with, 44
learning through research, 118
literature access, 95–100; company-wide request system for, 96–98; resources about, 158; search process recommended for, 98–100; summary of suggestions for, 95
literature reviews, 73, 142
Low, Adeline, 21n

M

manuscripts: article types for, 141–142; authorship considerations for, 147–148; blind review procedures for, 145; category requirements for, 135; decision types for, 150–151, 152; post-submission process for, 149–150; preparing for submission, 147; responding to decisions about, 151–152; submitting to journals, 148–149
McElroy, Alyssa, 21n
McKeown, Greg, 78, 162
meetings, RRC, 67–68
mentors, 122–132; characteristics of, 122; connecting with, 124–126; finding for your research, 123–124; maintaining the relationship with, 129–130; making the most of your time with, 127–129; offering yourself to others as, 131–132; organizing the relationship with, 126–127; resources

about, 157; transitioning out of the relationship with, 130–131
Miller, Keith, vii
mission statement, 140–141
mistakes, fear of making, 91–93
modeled prompts, 2
motivation deficits, 74–76
My Research Accomplishments worksheet, 34–37; blank form, 34–35; example answers, 36–37

N

National Mentoring Resource Center, 157
networking, 112–113, 157
Newport, Cal, 83, 162
newsletter writing, 137

O

obstacles to research, 17, 88–94; definition of barriers vs., 88; fear of making mistakes, 91–93; knowledge deficit, 88–91; research ideas deficit, 93–94. See also barriers to research
opportunities for research: expanding, 110–111; lack of, 94–95
ordering tasks, 85–86
organizational behavior management (OBM), 90
organizations: research policy for, 59–60; value of research to, 58–59
outlines, writing with/without, 133
out-of-date practices, 10
overthinking your writing, 133

P

pager prompts, 24–25
The PartnerShip, 100, 158
peer-review process, 139
persistence and patience, 109–110
personal benefits of publishing research, 31–42; career boost, 33–37; clinical practice improvements, 37–39; continuing education units, 42; ego boost, 31–33; fun, 41–42; questioning assumptions, 39–40

personal journal entries, 137
plagiarism: ethics code on, 47; scenario and recommendation, 50–51
planning process, 82–83
policy, research, 59–60
positive attitude, 136
practical strategies for research, 102–121; accomplishments review, 115–118; accountability to others, 120; building downtime into schedules, 114; contacting research contingencies, 109; creating a conducive work environment, 105–107; embedding research practices into clinical work, 108; expanding your research opportunities, 110–111; identifying research questions, 104; learning through your research, 118; making decisions about research, 102–104; mastering the art of imperfection, 108–109; networking and conferencing, 112–113; persistence and patience, 109–110; public speaking skills, 111–112; reading the literature, 105; setting bigger goals, 119; social interactions, 114–115; storytelling skills, 113
practitioner-researchers: fictional profiles of, 3–7; practice improvements among, 37–39; research role model for, 29–30. See also researchers
presentations, task analysis for, 81
problem behavior, resources on, 90
product reviews, 142
professional organizations, 155–156
ProQuest access, 98
PsychINFO subscriptions, 95, 96, 97
public speaking: developing skills in, 111–112; resources about, 157–158
Publication Manual of the American Psychological Association, 133, 163
PubMed Central access, 95
Purdue Online Writing Lab (OWL), 163

Q

questions: on choosing journals, 145–146; on choosing research topics, 12–14; on clinical practice improvements, 37–39; on considering your unique contribution, 20–21, 22–23; on ethical issues in research, 54; on fear of making mistakes, 92–93; on having fun in research work, 41–42; on helping consumers and general public, 25–26; on helping other researchers, 27–28; on personal progress/contributions, 31–33; on practice assumptions, 39–40; on research role modeling, 29–30; on skill vs. motivation deficits, 75; on work-life balance, 77

R

read-aloud reviews, 135
reading, importance of, 105
receptive language training, 10
regulations, complying with, 44
rejected papers: decision types for, 150–151, 152; staying positive about, 136, 152; task analysis for revising, 80
renewal and review process, 64–66; application example, 66; document example, 65
replications, published, 142
research: accountability in, 120; alternative types of, 73; author's journey with, 1–3; benefits of publishing, 19–43; choosing topics for, 11–14; clinical issues leading to, 14–16; contingencies for conducting, 109; environment conducive to, 105–107; ethical issues related to, 44–54; expanding your opportunities for, 110–111; gaining opportunities for, 94–95; generating ideas for, 93–94; learning continued through, 118; mentoring relationship for, 122–132; obstacles and barriers to, 17, 88–101; policy developed for, 59–60; practical strategies for, 102–121; study application for, 61

research articles, 141
Research Environment Worksheet, 107, 136
research policy template, 60
research renewal application, 66
research review committee (RRC), 55–72; annual renewal and review process, 64–66; approval requirement, 45, 52; consulting on research issues, 49; establishing for organizations, 56–72; informed consent document, 62; meeting time and structure, 67–68; overview description of, 55–56; research policy development, 59–60; researcher training process, 71–72; sample response letters from, 69–70; selecting and training members of, 57–58; speaking to organization leaders about, 58–59; study application development, 61; template for study-specific consent, 62–63
research study application, 61
researchers: accomplishments worksheet for, 34–37; alternative approaches to project work for, 76; research contributions helping other, 27–28; training process developed for, 71–72; unique and individual contributions of, 22–23. See also practitioner-researchers
ResearchGate website, 99
research-to-practice gap, 9–11; problems created by, 9–10; resources about, 158; solutions for bridging, 11
resources, 155–163; ABA journals/professional organizations, 155–156; on ethical issues, 156; on mentoring and networking, 157; on public speaking, 157–158; on research-to-practice gap, 158; on supervision, 159–161; on time management, 162; on writing, 163
resubmitting manuscripts, 150–151
resumes or CVs, 117
review of research: blind reviews, 145; ethics code related to, 45; renewal process and, 64–66; scenario and

recommendation, 51–52. See also research review committee
review papers, 142
reviewers, manuscript, 144
revisions: required by associate editors, 49–50; resubmitting manuscripts with, 150–151; task analysis for making, 80
Rice, Brian, 159
RRC. See research review committee

S

scenarios, research ethics, 48–54
schedules: downtime built into, 114; time management and, 83–84
searching the literature, 95, 98–100
self-care, importance of, 76–78
service delivery: ethics code on, 45; scenario and recommendation, 48–49
sign language, 2
Silvia, Paul, 83, 162
single-blind reviews, 145
single-subject design, 89
skill deficits, 74–75
social interactions, 114–115
sole authorship, 136–137
special interest groups (SIGs), 155, 156
special journal issues, 143
storytelling skills, 113, 135–136
supervision: author's research on, 118; mentoring relationship and, 129; resources about, 90, 159–161

T

tactile prompts, 24, 27
Tarbox, Jonathan, 143
target audience, 140
task analysis, 78–82; examples of using, 79–81; goal setting related to, 79, 81; ordering tasks for, 86
tasks: ordering work on, 85–86; process of analyzing, 78–82
technical/tutorial articles, 141
TED Talks, 157, 158
templates: research policy, 60; study-specific consent, 62–63

time blocking, 83
time-management strategies, 78–86; data-based decision making, 84–85; focusing on one project at a time, 86; ordering task lists, 85–86; planning and scheduling, 82–84; resources about, 162; task analysis, 78–82
to-do lists, 83
topics of research: process of choosing, 11–14; task analysis for developing, 80–81
training: researchers, 71–72; RRC members, 57–58
Treasure, Julian, 157
treatment models, 73
Trumpet Behavioral Health (TBH), 60, 64, 96

U

university IRBs, 72–73

V

Veazey, Sarah, 21n
verbal behavior: author's research on, 103; research articles on, 141; resources on, 90
Verbal Behavior Milestones Assessment and Placement Program (VBMAPP), 93
vibrating pagers, 24–25

W

website for book, 8
Women in Behavior Analysis (WIBA), 123–124, 157
work environment, 105–107
work-life balance, 76–78
worksheets: My Research Accomplishments, 34–35; Research Environment, 107, 136
writing: analyzing data about, 85; environment conducive to, 105–106, 136; resources about, 163; strategies for work and, 83; tips for process of, 133–137

MORE BOOKS from
NEW HARBINGER PUBLICATIONS

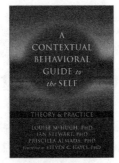
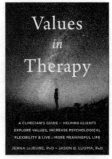

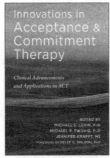

Did you know there are **free tools** you can download for this book?

Free tools are things like **worksheets**, **guided meditation exercises**, and **more** that will help you get the most out of your book.

You can download free tools for this book—whether you bought or borrowed it, in any format, from any source—from the New Harbinger website. All you need is a NewHarbinger.com account. Just use the URL provided in this book to view the free tools that are available for it. Then, click on the "download" button for the free tool you want, and follow the prompts that appear to log in to your NewHarbinger.com account and download the material.

You can also save the free tools for this book to your **Free Tools Library** so you can access them again anytime, just by logging in to your account! Just look for this button on the book's free tools page.

+ Save this to my free tools library

If you need help accessing or downloading free tools, visit **newharbinger.com/faq** or contact us at **customerservice@newharbinger.com.**